Generativ

From algorithms that draft clinical notes in seconds to autonomous agents that triage emergency room backlogs, artificial intelligence is quietly reshaping every facet of healthcare. *Generative AI: Unlocking the Next Chapter in Healthcare* is the first comprehensive guide to this revolution—charting how we got here, what's working now, and where the technology could take us next.

Drawing on frontline case studies from leading health systems, biotech labs, and tech giants, the book reveals how large language models, synthetic data engines, and multi-agent ecosystems are boosting diagnostic accuracy, accelerating drug discovery, and personalizing patient engagement. It also confronts the hard questions—privacy, bias, liability, and the fear of "machines taking over"—offering clear, actionable frameworks for ethical, human-centered deployment.

Written for clinicians, executives, innovators, and policy makers and patients alike, this definitive volume distils the expertise of industry pioneers into an accessible roadmap. You'll explore:

- The evolution from early machine learning to today's generative powerhouses
- Real world wins—ambient documentation, AI-assisted radiology, virtual nursing, and more
- The players shaping the landscape: Epic, Google, Microsoft, NVIDIA, Salesforce, and a wave of insurgent startups
- Guardrails that preserve trust, protect privacy, and keep humans in the loop
- Bold yet plausible futures—from digital twin medicine to globe-spanning agent networks

Whether you're leading a hospital, building health tech solutions, a tech startup, or simply curious about the future of care, *Generative AI: Unlocking the Next Chapter in Healthcare* delivers the insight, inspiration, and practical guidance you need to thrive in the era where human empathy and machine intelligence work side by side.

Generative AI
Unlocking the Next Chapter in Healthcare

Rohit Mahajan and Ritu M. Uberoy

Routledge
Taylor & Francis Group
A PRODUCTIVITY PRESS BOOK

Designed cover image: Shutterstock

First published 2026
by Routledge
605 Third Avenue, New York, NY 10158

and by Routledge
4 Park Square, Milton Park, Abingdon, Oxon, OX14 4RN

Routledge is an imprint of the Taylor & Francis Group, an informa business

ISBN: 9781041125693 (hbk)
ISBN: 9781041125679 (pbk)
ISBN: 9781003665434 (ebk)

DOI: 10.4324/9781003665434

Typeset in Garamond
by KnowledgeWorks Global Ltd.

Dedicated to all the Healthcare Leaders and Pioneers worldwide
your vision will light the path for a healthier world.

Contents

Acknowledgments

To our family and friends, whose unwavering support carried us through; to our colleagues, whose insights and encouragement enriched this journey; and to every healthcare professional who generously shared their time, stories, and expertise this book would not have been possible without you.

Foreword

Welcome to the Future of Healthcare Welcome to the Revolution

In the rapidly evolving landscape of healthcare, the integration of artificial intelligence (AI) is not just a possibility; it is an inevitability. As we stand on the brink of a new era, the potential of AI to revolutionize medicine is both exhilarating and daunting and necessary! *AI: Unlocking the Next Chapter in Healthcare* serves as a beacon and guidebook for those navigating this transformative journey, offering insights into the profound impact of large language models (LLMs) and generative AI (GAI) tools like ChatGPT or Gemini on the medical field.

The healthcare industry is no stranger to innovation. From the discovery of antibiotics to the development of minimally invasive surgical techniques, each advancement has been a stepping stone toward better patient outcomes and improved experiences. However, the advent of AI represents a paradigm shift unlike any other. It promises not only to enhance existing practices but to redefine the very fabric of healthcare delivery and research. While some technologies of the past never lived up to their hype, AI is likely to exceed the hype as we continue to execute on its promises.

This book is Rohit Mahajan and Ritu M. Uberoy's second exploration into the intersection of AI and healthcare. Following the success of *Quantum Care: A Deep Dive into AI for Health Delivery and Research*, they realized that healthcare practitioners required a roadmap and real-world examples from which to operate and draw inspiration. In this new volume, they delve deeper into the specific contributions of LLMs and GAI, technologies that are radically reshaping how we approach diagnostics, treatment planning, clinician experience, and patient engagement. These tools are not just augmenting human capabilities; they are expanding the boundaries of what is possible in medicine.

One of the core strengths of this book is its commitment to technical accuracy while maintaining an engaging and accessible narrative. It is designed to be a resource for a diverse audience, including physicians, healthcare administrators, technology executives, medical researchers, and administrators. By providing practical advice on GAI implementation and showcasing real-world case studies, the book equips readers with the knowledge needed to make informed decisions about integrating these technologies into their practices. The book helps readers move from the sidelines to the playing field.

Moreover, the book aims to inspire startups and innovators to join the healthcare GAI revolution. The potential applications of GAI in medicine are vast, from personalized medicine to voice to predictive analytics. The opportunities for innovation are limited only by our imagination. By highlighting successful implementations and featuring interviews with thought leaders, this book provides a roadmap for those looking to make a meaningful impact in this field. The book will at once motivate readers who are thinking about GAI to go for it, as well as encourage those readers who are just dreaming.

Each chapter is meticulously crafted to offer not only insights but also actionable takeaways. The inclusion of charts and graphics enhances understanding, while the commentary from Rohit, Ritu, and third-party experts provides a well-rounded perspective on the challenges and opportunities presented by GAI in healthcare. The structure of the book ensures a seamless transition from one chapter to the next, guiding readers through the complexities of GAI with clarity and precision.

As we embark on this exploration of AI's role in healthcare, it is important to acknowledge the ethical considerations and challenges that accompany such a transformative technology. The book does not shy away from these discussions, addressing issues such as data privacy, governance, algorithmic bias, and the need for robust regulatory frameworks. By confronting these challenges head-on, practitioners can ensure that the integration of AI into healthcare is both responsible and beneficial.

Generative AI: Unlocking the Next Chapter in Healthcare is more than just a book; it is a call to action. It invites readers to envision a future where AI is an integral part of healthcare, driving innovation, bettering experiences, and improving patient outcomes. A future where AI is part of the overall fabric of care. As we turn the page to this next era, let us embrace the possibilities that AI offers and work together to unlock its full potential in the world of medicine. This book is as practical as it gets.

Welcome to the future of healthcare. Welcome to the revolution.

Edward Marx
CEO, Marx Advisory
Author, Speaker & Consultant

Preface

Generative AI has the potential to change the world in ways that we can't even imagine. The future of generative AI is bright, and I'm excited to see what it will bring.

Bill Gates

I share Mr. Gates' enthusiasm about the promise of generative AI (GAI), and the pioneers in developing GAI tools, such as the now ubiquitous ChatGPT, indeed were able to imagine how it could change the world. However, they could not have expected how much and how quickly.

In my first book, *Quantum Care: A Deep Dive into AI for Health Delivery and Research,* which was published only a little over a year ago, ChatGPT was barely a blip on the radar. Now, here I am, writing a second book less than two years later about a technology that has made most of the AI and Machine Learning tools I wrote about in my first book obsolete!

Another thing that has changed since my first book is that I am proud to collaborate on this one with Ritu M. Uberoy. She has two degrees in computer science, and her Master's is from Santa Clara University in California, so she spent many years in the Bay Area in the heart of Silicon Valley. In bringing this book to life, she and I were driven by a shared desire to illuminate the complex facets of GAI and its impact on healthcare. Ritu's deep understanding of the hands-on user experience seamlessly integrates with my own experience in development and implementation. This allowed us to present a comprehensive and nuanced analysis that would not have been possible without our collaborative approach. Throughout this book, our voices will be woven together. Sometimes, I, Rohit, will be identified as the speaker, sometimes Ritu, and other times, it will be "we" for our collaborative insights.

As co-authors, we've come together to share our collective experiences and insights into GAI in healthcare. Ritu serves as the co-host of *The Big Unlock*—a widely followed podcast that features insightful conversations with healthcare CIOs, CDOs, and other senior leaders. Through these dialogues, she explores critical trends shaping the digital health landscape, including Voice Agents, Agentic AI, GenAI, digital front doors, and data-driven care delivery. With my own focus on startups and implementation, I observed firsthand what could both empower and hinder progress. Through this book, together, we aim to bridge these perspectives and offer readers a comprehensive view of the challenges and opportunities created by GAI in healthcare.

Why This Book and Why Now?

Generative AI literally gives anyone the ability to be more productive at what they do. That is true not only in their working lives. Whether you are planning a vacation, your two-year-old's birthday party, or investigating a new drug, GAI lets you do it faster, more accurately, and more efficiently. These large language models (LLMs) have ingested the world's knowledge in every available human language. That is remarkable in its power and scope. It touches all walks of life. It's touching filmmaking, it's touching book writing, it's touching anything that you do in your work or personal life.

You don't need any specialized programming language to access GAI, which democratizes it for a lot of people. It is similar to the move from mainframe computers—large machines operated only by highly technical experts—to personal computers, which anyone could use.

The other reason it has become so pervasive is that it does not dominate only one field. It has applications and solutions across design, media, healthcare, academia, and business. This is one of the first digital tools of its power that literally is available to everybody and can make you better at what you do, no matter what you do. Obviously, nobody wants to feel like they are missing out or being left behind, so everyone wants to jump on the GAI bandwagon. If your business is not using ChatGPT or similar tools as you are reading this preface, we bet it will be by the time you get to the last chapter!

As Ritu has put it, there is no doubt that Gen AI is the future. It is already changing how companies do business and how people interact with companies they do business with. Every sector has to think about alternative business models and how they will approach this powerful new technology. Some organizations are still far behind; some are further along in their approach. A lot of innovation and disruption is being done by startups.

We want readers to understand that GAI is not just a futuristic concept but a present-day reality reshaping healthcare. Whether you are a clinician, researcher, or healthcare entrepreneur, our goal is to provide actionable knowledge, inspire innovation, and foster informed discussions around the ethical deployment of AI in medicine.

Our Early Impressions of ChatGPT: Tool or Toy?

Having already been working in AI implementation for healthcare for several years before ChatGPT came on the scene, we were already quite familiar with how natural language processing (NLP) was driving innovation in AI for healthcare. NLP is what made healthcare such a match for traditional AI in the first place, and now an industry that has the most to benefit from advanced GAI. When you think about it, most biomedical information is out there in unstructured formats such as doctors' notes, hospital admission records, coroner's reports, patient anecdotes, and so on. This makes sifting through that data for "medical detective work," be that diagnostics or drug discovery, quite difficult. When coupled with NLP algorithms, AI offers a powerful solution to this problem. With NLP, AI algorithms are being written that can analyze documents and other datasets and identify biologically relevant text elements. Couple that with LLMs, and you have a digital tool that was almost made for the healthcare industry. Which brings us to ChatGPT.

As soon as we heard about ChatGPT and could begin to play with it for ourselves, we immediately saw that this was no toy and it had the power to fundamentally transform healthcare by fulfilling the promises that NLP brought to the table. I was at a medical conference; as I relate this story, you will understand why I cannot provide more details than that. At the conference my team and I attended, there was a call for abstracts. One of the abstracts discussed how pharmaceutical companies could utilize the CRM tool Salesforce to better engage with key opinion leaders, typically physicians. We had recently hired someone on the AI side of things, and I got together with this person. What we wound up doing, at his suggestion—just as an experiment, mind you—was feeding the parameters of the abstract into ChatGPT. After tweaking the prompts a few times, we came up with something we liked. We submitted that abstract to the panel, and it got selected! The entire process took less than half an hour, and we really did not even do the task!

You have to understand that this was a technical abstract that cleared a panel of pharmaceutical researchers, and they had no idea that ChatGPT had helped us write a good portion of it.

From generating that abstract in less than thirty minutes to medical summaries to aiding in literature reviews, it became clear that this technology was more than a novelty—it was a tool with real-world applications. We recognized the profound potential for GAI to streamline workflows, enhance diagnostics, and empower healthcare professionals globally. This book reflects our collective insights from the front lines of this technological shift.

A New Way of Doing Things

If we want our readers to take but one insight from this book, it is that GAI is not just about productivity gains or improving efficiencies. It's about an entirely new way of doing things. That applies to healthcare, medical research, and every other commercial or personal use of generative AI.

If you are not already using ChatGPT or similar Gen AI tools, we urge you to do so. Everyone should experiment with it. Anyone reading this book should also keep abreast of the latest developments in GAI because things are changing fast and will continue to evolve, at least for some period of time, until they stabilize. And, finally, if you read my first book or this one because you are entrepreneurially inclined and focused on healthcare, understand that there is a tremendous opportunity for startups to disrupt this very dynamic industry segment.

A Modern Prometheus

Some might argue that putting GAI's power into the general public's hands was much like Prometheus giving fire to mankind. The same has been said of many technological advancements, from electricity to nuclear power to computers themselves.

Still, the analogy comparing Generative AI to Prometheus is compelling, highlighting both the immense potential and the inherent risks associated with powerful technologies. Just as fire can warm and illuminate or destroy and consume, generative AI has the capacity to bring about tremendous advancements and, if misused, can lead to significant issues.

I would respond to this analogy by emphasizing the importance of *intent, responsibility, and governance* in wielding these new tools. Fire, in the myth, wasn't inherently good or bad—it depended entirely on how it was used and controlled. Similarly, AI itself is neutral; it's the purposes for which it's employed and the frameworks that surround its development and application that determine whether it's a force for positive change or a source of harm.

Generative AI has the potential to revolutionize industries, amplify creativity, democratize access to information, and solve complex problems. But it also presents risks, such as misinformation, loss of privacy, and ethical dilemmas, that must be navigated carefully. Thus, the analogy is apt: just as mankind learned to regulate fire, harnessing its power for the common good, society must establish norms, standards, and ethical guidelines for AI.

Ultimately, the challenge is to ensure that the "fire" of AI is shared in a way that maximizes benefits while minimizing harm, fostering a balance between innovation and caution, between empowerment and responsibility.

Together, Ritu and I hope to inspire new ways of thinking about both the promises and the challenges created by Generative AI for healthcare and provide practical strategies for successful implementation and public confidence. We're excited to share this journey with you.

Introduction

Generative models are changing the way we think about machine intelligence and creativity, and have the potential to transform industries from media to finance to healthcare.

Oriol Vinyals, Principal Scientist at Google DeepMind

The transformative potential of generative AI (GAI) is becoming increasingly apparent across many sectors, but its impact on healthcare stands out as particularly revolutionary. GAI refers to the use of machine learning models, such as large language models (LLMs), which are designed to generate new data, including text, images, and even molecular structures, that can mimic or build upon existing information. These technologies are not only redefining how we think about artificial intelligence but are also paving the way for unprecedented advancements in medical care.

In healthcare, GAI holds the promise of transforming everything from diagnostics and personalized treatment plans to drug discovery and patient care management. Large language models, a core aspect of GAI, excel in natural language understanding and generation, allowing them to process vast amounts of unstructured data, such as medical records, research papers, and clinical trial results. This capability has already begun to change how healthcare professionals access and interpret complex medical information, leading to faster, more accurate decision-making.

The importance of GAI in healthcare cannot be overstated. As the demands on healthcare systems continue to grow, driven by aging populations, rising healthcare costs, and the increasing complexity of diseases, GAI offers scalable solutions that enhance both the efficiency and quality of care. GAI models, for example, can analyze medical images, pathology slides, and genomic data with unmatched accuracy, enabling earlier detection of conditions such as cancer. Furthermore, they can simulate chemical interactions and design novel molecules, dramatically reducing the time and cost associated with drug development.

From analyzing medical images to discovering new drug compounds, GAI is at the forefront of innovation, offering powerful tools that can significantly improve patient outcomes.

What Is GAI?

Generative artificial intelligence (GAI) refers to a subset of AI that uses neural networks to generate content, such as text, images, or even entire applications, autonomously. GAI models, like ChatGPT, are trained on vast datasets and can produce human-like content.

GAI relies on deep learning techniques, including neural networks with multiple layers. It leverages natural language processing (NLP), computer vision, and other AI technologies. In CRM, GAI applications often involve chatbots, predictive analytics, and automated content generation.

The Relationship Between GAI and "Traditional AI"

In the brief time since GAI has come on the scene, it would seem that it has supplanted "traditional" artificial intelligence. In fact, we are at a point where those of us in the business are talking about the difference between "legacy machine learning" and GAI solutions. However, one should not picture the progression as being so linear with GAI, like a layer or evolutionary strata on top of traditional AI. The relationship is more of one of concentric circles, with one growing out from the other like ripples after a rock is tossed into a pond.

The breakthroughs and advances that we have right now in Gen AI may seem to have been built directly on top of machine learning and traditional AI, but it has not replaced them by any means. It is more like branches from the same root. GAI leverages the underlying neural networks and the systems from traditional ML and AI, but it has taken them in a different direction with a divergent purpose.

GAI is very good at communication, creative pursuits, and helping researchers think outside of the box and find the proverbial needle in a haystack. Traditional AI algorithms are still very good at their original purpose—scanning massive databases and predicting outcomes. That is not going to go away. While generative AI opens new areas for innovation and utilization, it complements rather than replaces the ubiquity of existing ML and deep learning models, each serving distinct roles within the IT environment.

Importance of GAI in Healthcare

The importance of GAI in healthcare cannot be overstated. From accelerating drug discovery to enhancing diagnostic accuracy, GAI drives innovation, reduces costs, and improves patient outcomes. As healthcare systems grapple worldwide with increasing demand and limited resources, GAI offers scalable solutions to some of the most pressing challenges in the sector.

In a field where human error can have life-or-death consequences, the accuracy and reliability of GAI offer a significant advantage. AI tools can serve as a second set of "eyes" for radiologists or help pharmacists identify potential drug interactions. They can also revolutionize medical training by simulating real-world scenarios, allowing healthcare professionals to practice complex procedures or decision-making in a safe, controlled environment.

GAI, like traditional AI, is already having a profound impact on diagnostics and treatment, but some of the capabilities unique to GAI allow it to improve healthcare delivery in several other quite significant ways. Any healthcare provider or medical facility administrator will tell you we are facing a severe nursing shortage in this country. LLMs can help solve this problem with "virtual nurses." The aim is to create virtual nurses for chronic care that use an automated "voice" to speak to and listen to patients. Although virtual nurses will not be involved in clinical diagnosis, they can remind patients to take their medicine, follow through with care plans, schedule follow-up appointments, review medication issues, and help patients navigate care-access issues.

Hippocratic AI is already developing such "virtual nurses."

GAI solutions are poised to create huge efficiencies for clinicians by liberating them from their keyboards. LLMs could also prove good at checking in with patients with chronic conditions during the time between conventional encounters with caregivers, writing notes in patients' records, and summarizing patients' issues. All of this makes care much faster and allows physicians to spend more time with their patients.

Such musings are far from academic. In June of 2024, Oracle Computer announced the launch of its Clinical Digital Assistant, a GAI-powered solution that uses voice recognition technology to record key elements of the physician-patient encounter, interpret the information, and then accurately input a draft of the typical doctor's notes into the Oracle Health EHR. The physician can then quickly review and approve the clinical documentation produced. According to the company's website, the "Oracle Health Clinical AI Agent provides a comprehensive mobile solution that helps physicians navigate workflow challenges—supporting time- and cost-efficient operations—by combining the capabilities of clinical automation, note generation, integrated dictation, and proposed actions in a single, unified experience."

In a press release announcing the launch of the AI Agent, Oracle said, "Early adopters report game-changing results, saving 20-40% in documentation time."

Oracle is not alone. Many of the best-known tech giants are betting that Gen AI will be the key to unlocking innovation within the healthcare industry. Google, NVIDIA, Insilco, and, of course, Open AI all have skin in the game.

A Word about Healthcare GAI and the Potential for Startups

If the early adopters are any indication, the healthcare industry stands out as an exceptional opportunity for startups and investors focused on GAI solutions due to its pressing need for innovation and its inherent complexity. The challenges faced by healthcare—ranging from aging populations and rising costs to an increasing prevalence of chronic diseases—demand creative solutions. Generative AI is already playing a transformative role here by improving diagnostics, accelerating drug discovery, and enhancing the precision of medical care.

One of healthcare's greatest assets and challenges is the vast amount of data it generates daily. Electronic health records, medical imaging, genomic data, and patient-generated information from wearables present a data goldmine for GAI applications. These technologies can unlock insights from complex datasets that are otherwise too intricate for human analysis, enabling breakthroughs in personalized medicine. By integrating disparate data sources, AI can create highly individualized treatment plans tailored to each patient's unique profile.

Cost inefficiencies and resource constraints also make healthcare ripe for disruption. Administrative burdens, staff shortages, and wasted resources can be mitigated by generative AI, which automates repetitive tasks such as medical transcription, claims processing, and appointment scheduling. Additionally, GAI tools can enhance clinical decision-making by synthesizing vast volumes of research and clinical guidelines into actionable recommendations. By reducing the burden on healthcare workers, these tools not only save time but also improve patient outcomes.

The adoption of digital health solutions has surged, particularly in the wake of the COVID-19 pandemic, creating a fertile landscape for GAI-driven innovation. Startups are building on this momentum by developing GAI-LLM-powered platforms that expand access to care, especially in underserved or remote areas. For example, AI chatbots can triage patients and provide immediate guidance, while mental health apps offer scalable and affordable therapy options to address a growing demand.

Regulatory and reimbursement advances have further fueled the appeal of healthcare AI for startups. Governments and regulatory bodies, recognizing the potential of GAI, have begun crafting frameworks to streamline its approval and deployment in healthcare settings. Value-based care models, which tie payments to patient outcomes, are also incentivizing the adoption of GAI solutions that improve efficiency and quality of care.

On a global scale, healthcare's universal need presents opportunities for startups to address disparities and scale solutions to diverse markets. Gen AI can make healthcare more accessible and equitable, such as by enabling cost-effective tools for low-resource settings or facilitating multilingual communication between patients and providers. The integration of AI with emerging technologies like robotics and wearables adds another dimension to this opportunity, offering new ways to deliver precision care and real-time interventions.

For startups, the convergence of these factors creates an extraordinary opportunity to deliver meaningful solutions while capturing a share of the massive healthcare market. Investors are drawn to the high-growth potential of this sector, and startups can carve out niches by addressing specific pain points, such as rare disease identification or administrative inefficiencies. Collaboration with hospitals, research institutions, and pharmaceutical companies can further improve the impact and scalability of these solutions. In healthcare, generative AI not only holds the promise of financial success but also the power to transform lives on a global scale.

Current and Future Investment in Gen AI Solutions for Healthcare

The investment landscape for generative AI (GAI) solutions in healthcare is experiencing significant growth, reflecting the technology's transformative potential in the sector. In 2022, the global GAI healthcare market was valued at approximately $1.6 billion. Projections indicate a robust expansion, with expectations to reach around $30.4 billion by 2032, corresponding to a compound annual growth rate (CAGR) of 34.9% over the forecast period.

According to Allied Market Research's Generative AI in Healthcare Market Report, 2023–2032, in the US, the GAI healthcare market was estimated at $518.4 million in 2023. It is anticipated to grow at a CAGR of 36.4% from 2024 to 2030, driven by increasing awareness and adoption of AI technologies in healthcare settings.

These projections are supported by Grand View Research's US Healthcare Generative AI Market Trends report, which indicated substantial investments in the sector. For instance, in 2024, Cera, a UK-based healthcare startup, achieved unicorn status with a valuation exceeding $1 billion after raising $150 million.

The funds are intended to enhance Cera's AI technology aimed at reducing hospitalizations and falls among the elderly, as well as to expand home care services. Additionally, according to the same report, in October 2023, the US National Science Foundation announced an investment of $10.9 million in research to implement generative AI technologies, underscoring America's commitment to advancing AI applications in healthcare.

These statistics and investments highlight a dynamic and rapidly evolving market, presenting significant opportunities for startups and investors focusing on GAI solutions tailored to healthcare.

The Promise and the Reality: Challenges Remain

We cannot stress enough the unbridled potential for GAI in healthcare—it is vast enough to fill a book! However, while we are excited about the possibilities, the large-scale implementation of GAI still faces a myriad of challenges, many of which stem from the unique sensitivities and complexities of the healthcare field.

One of the foremost issues is data privacy and security. Healthcare data is highly sensitive and subject to stringent regulations like HIPAA in the US, so ensuring that AI systems do not inadvertently expose or misuse patient information is critical. Additionally, there is a concern about the reliability and bias of generative AI models. These tools are only as good as the data they are trained on, and biases in training datasets can lead to inequities in care or inaccuracies in medical advice, potentially putting lives at risk. Trust is another major hurdle; healthcare professionals and patients alike may question the reliability of AI-generated insights, especially in critical decision-making scenarios where a wrong diagnosis or treatment recommendation could have severe consequences. There is also the challenge of integration—healthcare systems often operate on legacy software and infrastructure, making it difficult to implement cutting-edge AI technologies seamlessly. Power consumption is another issue; advanced GAI systems require huge "data farms," which consume enormous amounts of power. Finally, regulatory and ethical considerations present a significant barrier as governing bodies struggle to keep up with the rapid pace of GAI advancements, leaving developers and practitioners navigating a gray area of compliance and responsibility.

The tech industry is actively working with healthcare to address these challenges through a variety of approaches. To tackle privacy concerns, there has been a growing emphasis on federated learning and advanced encryption techniques, which allow AI systems to learn from data without exposing sensitive information. Bias mitigation is being pursued by diversifying training datasets and incorporating fairness algorithms to ensure AI tools provide equitable outcomes across diverse populations. To build trust, companies are prioritizing transparency by developing explainable AI (XAI) systems that provide clear reasoning for their outputs, making it easier for healthcare providers to understand and validate AI-generated recommendations. Integration challenges are being met with scalable, cloud-based solutions and APIs designed to interface with existing healthcare infrastructures. The industry is collaborating with policymakers and healthcare organizations on the regulatory front to establish robust guidelines and frameworks that balance innovation with safety and compliance.

By addressing these hurdles head-on, the tech industry is working to create a future where generative AI can enhance healthcare delivery without compromising safety, equity, or trust.

Throughout the book, we will discuss these challenges and address them all and more in greater detail in Chapter 6.

About the Authors

Rohit Mahajan is a digital health entrepreneur and author of the #1 Amazon bestseller *Quantum Care: A Deep Dive into AI for Health Delivery and Research.* He is the CEO of BigRio and Damo and the Founder of Saviance Technologies. Rohit co-hosts *The Big Unlock* podcast and was honored with the 2025 GHLF Global Impact Award for Digital Health Innovation. A Wharton Fellow and HBS graduate, he has completed advanced AI and healthcare programs from MIT and Harvard. His work focuses on using technology to drive compassionate, equitable, and impactful healthcare transformation.

Ritu M. Uberoy is a technology executive, entrepreneur, and educator with 25+ years of experience in digital transformation across healthcare and life sciences. She leads the Generative AI Center of Excellence at BigRio and the DigiMTM initiative at Damo Consulting. Ritu hosts *The Big Unlock* podcast and regularly conducts GenAI workshops for healthcare leaders. She holds degrees from NSIT and Santa Clara University and has completed executive programs at Harvard, MIT, and Wharton. Her forthcoming book offers senior healthcare and pharma executives a practical roadmap to implementing generative AI.

Chapter 1

Evolution of AI in Healthcare: From ML to LLMs

The day healthcare can fully embrace AI is the day we have a revolution in terms of cutting costs and improving care.

Fei-Fei Li

Introduction: The Rise of AI in Healthcare

Artificial intelligence (AI) has long held the promise of transforming healthcare by automating routine tasks, enhancing diagnostic capabilities, and improving patient outcomes. However, the journey from early AI applications to today's large language models (LLMs) and Gen AI solutions has been both complex and dynamic. What began as basic machine learning (ML) algorithms focused on analyzing structured data has now evolved into sophisticated systems capable of understanding, generating, and even reasoning with natural language.

Healthcare, in general, and clinical medicine, specifically, is very interesting in that, more so than any other industry, it is equal parts science, technology, and human interaction. This is what makes it so ripe for what can be created with natural language processing (NLP) and Gen AI. Those first two parts of the "cocktail"—science and technology—have been covered by traditional or

DOI: 10.4324/9781003665434-1

legacy AI, and generative AI (GAI) completes the mix by covering the human side. Then you have the non-clinical aspects of healthcare that are very human-centric, administration, finance, customer service, resource allocation, etc., and it is very easy to envision how successful implementation of GAI solutions can leapfrog from clinical applications into these other areas.

We were recently in consultation with Northwell Health, one of the largest healthcare providers in the Northeastern US, and besides the obvious cases in which you might think they were or wanted to leverage GAI solutions, they told us how they were using Gen AI in their sustainability efforts and making sure they meet with New York state carbon footprint requirements. They are a huge healthcare system dealing with upwards of 50,000–80,000 vendors, and they have to make sure that whatever they are buying from these suppliers will keep them below their sustainability targets. You can imagine that with so much variability from copy machines to high-tech medical equipment, it could be a near-impossible task for human environmental engineers, but it was simple to create a GAI-driven survey that could provide the proper analysis quickly and efficiently.

Historical Overview: AI's Early Applications in Healthcare

The roots of AI in healthcare can be traced back to the early days of ML in the 1970s and 1980s, when algorithms were first applied to process clinical data and develop diagnostic tools. Early AI systems were rule-based expert systems designed to mimic human decision-making. Systems like MYCIN, developed in the 1970s at Stanford University, used a set of rules to diagnose and recommend treatments for bacterial infections, demonstrating the early potential of AI in healthcare.

However, these early systems were limited by the computational power and algorithmic approaches of the time. They could only handle structured data, such as laboratory results or patient demographics, and often required extensive input from human experts to function properly. This reliance on structured, curated data slowed the adoption of AI in many areas of healthcare.

In the 2000s, ML techniques, particularly supervised learning, began to demonstrate more practical applications in healthcare. These systems could analyze large datasets and recognize patterns that were previously difficult for human experts to detect. For instance, algorithms developed to predict patient outcomes, such as the likelihood of readmission or disease progression, started to gain traction. Hospitals and clinics adopted predictive analytics to improve patient care, optimize resource allocation, and streamline operations.

One of the major breakthroughs came with the advent of NLP, a subset of AI that allows computers to understand, interpret, and respond to human language. In healthcare, NLP became a game-changer by enabling systems to analyze unstructured data, such as physician notes, clinical narratives, and research papers. Early NLP applications made it possible to automate the extraction of clinical insights from electronic health records (EHRs), improving the accuracy of diagnosis and enhancing decision support systems. This capability laid the groundwork for more advanced AI applications, particularly as healthcare began generating enormous amounts of unstructured data in the form of medical notes, research articles, and clinical trial reports.

For example, NLP has been employed in patient care to analyze clinical documentation and flag potential medical errors, aiding in quality control and compliance. In diagnostics, it has helped in the interpretation of radiology reports and pathology slides, offering more efficient and precise results. NLP applications like IBM Watson Health made headlines by assisting physicians in diagnosing rare diseases by rapidly synthesizing information from medical journals, clinical trials, and patient records.

These early successes paved the way for even more sophisticated AI tools, particularly the emergence of GAI models like LLMs, which have revolutionized the way AI interacts with human language.

The Shift to Generative AI and LLMs

While traditional AI models, such as ML algorithms and early NLP tools, were impressive, they lacked the ability to generate content and context with the fluidity and understanding seen in human interactions. This is where GAI, particularly LLMs like GPT-3 and GPT-4 entered the scene.

The defining feature of GAI is its ability to create new data, including human-like text, based on the vast datasets on which it has been trained. LLMs such as GPT-4 are designed to understand context, predict future text based on prior input, and generate content that is coherent and contextually relevant. This has transformative implications for healthcare, where language plays a crucial role in diagnosis, treatment, research, and patient communication.

For Example, NVIDIA, in collaboration with Hippocratic AI, has created virtual nursing assistants that have outperformed their human counterparts in early testing. The major chip company's "AI-Agents" were the brainchild of a collaboration with Hippocratic AI. The so-called healthcare agents have already been shown to outperform other LLMs as well as human nurses in specific tasks.

Generative AI vs Traditional AI: Why the Difference Matters

The shift from traditional AI techniques such as ML and deep learning (DL) to GAI is not just an evolution of technology, it also represents a fundamental paradigm shift in how AI interacts with the healthcare system.

Traditional AI, including ML and DL, operates by learning patterns from historical data and applying those patterns to new data. For instance, an ML model might learn from thousands of chest X-rays to identify pneumonia in new X-rays. While effective, these systems are typically confined to very specific tasks. They cannot generate new insights outside of their training parameters, nor can they engage in meaningful dialogue with healthcare providers or patients.

GAI, and particularly LLMs, extend these capabilities by not only analyzing data but also creating new content based on that analysis. This ability is profoundly important in healthcare because of the unstructured nature of much of the medical information—clinical notes, research articles, patient interactions, and more. Unlike traditional AI, which requires structured input, LLMs can analyze, synthesize, and even generate human-like responses based on vast datasets of unstructured information.

The difference between these two types of AI also becomes apparent when looking at scalability. Traditional AI models often require painstaking human intervention to update and refine them, especially when new medical knowledge becomes available. GAI models, on the other hand, can be trained on continuously evolving datasets and can immediately incorporate the latest research findings, making them much more adaptable to the fast-paced world of healthcare.

This adaptability is particularly useful in areas like medical research, diagnostics, and treatment planning, where the landscape is rapidly evolving, and staying current with the latest discoveries is critical for effective patient care.

It's a Matter of Time

Perhaps the most valuable advantage GAI brings to medicine over traditional AI is the gift of time. When was the last time you went to see your doctor? How long did you wait despite having an appointment an hour or more? And when you finally got in to see him or her, how much time did he or she have to spend with you? Less than you would have liked, we are sure!

Doctors everywhere are over-booked and short-staffed. Every single practitioner we have ever spoken with says they wish they could spend more quality time with their patients—if they could, but paperwork burdens, staffing issues, and other administrative details simply make it impossible. It was not always like this.

You may have still spent longer than you would like in the waiting room, but once you got to see the doctor, things were quite different. If you are of a certain generation, as Ritu and I are, you can easily remember a time when you would go to see the doctor, and your visit was far more personal than it is now.

The doctor would look you in the eye, ask how you were doing, and genuinely listen to your concerns. There was no computer screen or tablet between you and the doctor, no hurried typing to distract from your interaction. The visit consisted of jotted notes on a legal pad combined with a genuine human connection that's hard to find in today's clinics.

So, what changed?

As technology advanced, we embraced electronic medical records (EMRs) and digital documentation. This shift brought many benefits. We reduced medication errors and improved access to patient history, and we could use this digital data to track disease and public health trends. Prescriptions could be sent electronically to pharmacies, lab results became easier to track, and, overall, the health system became more efficient.

However, these improvements came with a price.

In order to get the most out of EMRs and the shift to digital health, documentation needed to become highly structured and detailed. This meant physicians had to spend more time entering data into systems, time often taken away from face-to-face interactions with patients. Doctors found themselves clicking away at keyboards during appointments, making patients feel like they were competing with a screen for their provider's attention. The personal connection that once was the cornerstone of medical care began to all but disappear, replaced by the eerie glow of a monitor and the clatter of keys.

According to recent studies, over 80% of patients say the biggest problem with their healthcare experience is poor communication, particularly in the exam room. However, GAI is now changing all of that for the better.

Providers recognize these problems and have always said it was one of time management. They must spend endless hours filling out forms, patient notes, writing prescriptions, etc. All of which takes quality time away from patient interaction. In fact, one of the most pressing topics impacting healthcare conversations today is physician burnout. Recent surveys have found that providers spend as much as five hours a day performing administrative tasks.

But GAI is changing all of that. LLM-driven GAI tools are streamlining many of these tedious and time-consuming processes, allowing doctors to focus more on care.

Case in point. John Muir Health (JMH), a not-for-profit health system in Walnut Creek, California, is pioneering the use of GAI to address this critical and growing challenge in healthcare. In partnership with Ambience Healthcare, JMH deployed Ambient "AI scribes" to help reduce clinician burnout, improve documentation efficiency, and enhance patient care—ultimately delivering measurable clinical and financial value.

In early 2023, JMH ranked in the bottom 10th percentile nationally for time spent in notes among Epic users. Providers were spending an average of 7.1 minutes per 15-minute visit documenting, reducing face-to-face time with patients, and driving dissatisfaction. A survey revealed that 73% of JMH providers were experiencing at least one symptom of burnout—well above the national average of 48%.

Faced with rising clinician fatigue and documentation inefficiencies, JMH leadership identified ambient "AI scribes" as a high-potential solution. The goal is to reduce documentation time, restore clinician-patient connection, and enable providers to focus more on care, not clicks.

"JMH moved quickly to explore Ambient AI technology. Clinicians participated in live simulations with real patient scenarios—including complex pediatric and inpatient encounters—to evaluate vendors. Ambience Healthcare stood out for its note quality and ability to parse out who was speaking," said Dr. Priti Patel, Chief Medical Information Officer, John Muir Health System

JMH collaborated with Ambience to build a custom, bidirectional integration with Epic, using SmartLinks and mobile apps. This integration allowed AI-generated notes to be embedded directly into standard workflows, customized by specialty and provider preferences. Patient instructions and assessment plans were also generated based on AI interpretation of the encounter. This change unlocked massive interest: over 100 providers signed up within weeks.

"John Muir Health's ambient AI initiative shows how strategic deployment of GenAI can enhance clinical workflows, reduce burnout, and improve both provider and patient experience," Dr. Patel concluded. "Through strong leadership, stakeholder engagement, technical integration, and thoughtful change management, JMH transformed a challenging documentation burden into a success story—laying the groundwork for future AI-driven transformation."

Ambient Listening

As you can see from the JMH example cited above, ambient listening technology has been a real game changer. Ambient listening is a GAI tool that has removed the need for notetaking during an appointment. With ambient listening, providers can record the appointment and review a conversation draft summary. The summary easily integrates into the patient's progress note and recommends the next steps. This removes the device barrier, freeing the provider to spend more "stethoscope time" with patients, meaning additional time for the physical examination, with the additional time savings and reduced administrative workload.

Ambient listening uses voice recognition to record and transcribe conversations between doctors and patients in real-time, essentially acting as a digital scribe, allowing doctors to focus more fully on their patients during appointments by automatically generating clinical notes instead of manually documenting information, thus freeing up their time to engage more deeply with the patient.

The technology listens to the conversation and extracts key medical information to create a draft of the patient's medical record, reducing the need for manual notetaking. By minimizing the need to look at a computer during a consultation, doctors can maintain better eye contact and focus on the patient's concerns. It also means doctors spend less time on paperwork after appointments, and it is helping to alleviate patient burnout, giving them back more personal time.

Ambient listening saves time for practitioners and money for healthcare administrators. Doctors love it, patients love it, and even CEOs and CFOs love it. It is the ultimate healthcare GAI win-win. We have interviewed doctors who told us that if they are offered a job opportunity with any given healthcare facility or organization, one of the first questions before going any further is whether they are using ambient listening because they consider it a condition for hire!

"I see tremendous opportunity in ambient technologies—tools that can passively listen, transcribe, and intelligently summarize clinical conversations in real time," said Crystal Broj, Enterprise Chief Digital Transformation Officer, Medical University of South Carolina. "These solutions reduce the documentation burden on providers, giving them back time for what matters most: patient care."

As AI first started to be adopted by the healthcare industry, there was a fear among patients and providers that it could reduce human interaction at the point of care. However, now that AI and, particularly, GAI are becoming more commonplace, studies have found that quite the opposite is true. By reducing the administrative and paperwork burden, AI is actually helping practitioners spend more quality time with patients. It is also making up for terrible staffing shortages and reducing employee burnout among healthcare workers.

A recent study published by Google Cloud and The Harris Poll sheds light on the extent of this burden—and it also highlights how GAI can help.

The study found that healthcare professionals are open to using GAI, with 91% of providers and 97% of payors saying they feel positive about AI's potential to ease administrative burdens. The general public feels the same, with 72% of respondents saying using AI is a worthwhile way to allow their healthcare providers more time to talk to them. Here are a few ways gen AI can help accomplish that:

- Making it easier to search patient documents and medical records
- Creating clinical documents, like discharge summaries, progress notes, and referral letters, gives clinicians more time to focus on reviewing and finalizing the documents
- Getting prior authorizations approved faster by pre-populating forms, flagging potential issues, and suggesting relevant clinical guidelines
- Speeding up turnaround times in medical imaging by creating initial drafts of reports, allowing radiologists to prioritize complex cases and collaborate more effectively

This is reflective of the current trend in AI for healthcare, where it is now generally accepted by practitioners and administrators alike that GAI is not here to replace human compassion and expertise in healthcare; instead, it can augment that by allowing professionals to focus more on people, not paperwork.

Rather than the initial fears that "machines will replace us" in healthcare, the report and our personal experience indicate that GAI can pave the way to a more efficient, accurate, and human-centered system where the needs of patients are always at the forefront.

The Emergence of GAI and Its Impact on Medical Practice and Research

GAI has already begun reshaping both clinical practice and medical research in profound ways. For instance, LLMs are now being used to assist in clinical decision-making by providing evidence-based treatment options, synthesizing patient data with the latest research, and even drafting detailed patient care plans.

One of the earliest and most impactful uses of LLMs in healthcare has been in automating the summarization of patient records and clinical notes. As mentioned above, companies like Nuance Communications have leveraged ambient listening technologies and married them with GAI to develop systems that listen to doctor-patient conversations and automatically generate concise, accurate clinical documentation. This not only reduces the administrative burden on healthcare providers but also improves the accuracy of medical records.

Beyond medical documentation, the other area of clinical medicine where GAI is having a profound impact is in diagnostics and medical decision-making. GAI is now being used to assist in diagnostics by synthesizing medical knowledge from vast datasets. For instance, LLMs can rapidly analyze millions of research papers, clinical trial results, and patient data to suggest potential diagnoses and treatment options. In one case, GPT-based models were trained to assist radiologists by offering contextual insights about abnormalities found in imaging results.

A little lesser-known application of GAI, but one that is making an equally huge impact, is in leveraging LLM technology in the mental health arena. For example, chatbot applications powered by LLMs are being used in mental health and patient communication. For example, Woebot Health has deployed an AI-based mental health chatbot that engages users in therapeutic conversations, providing support and counseling based on cognitive-behavioral therapy techniques. The chatbot's ability to generate relevant responses in real-time showcases how LLMs can help bridge the gap in patient care when human resources are scarce.

In medical research, GAI is accelerating drug discovery by predicting the efficacy of new compounds, analyzing the interactions of drugs at a molecular level, and identifying new targets for therapeutic intervention. The ability of AI to process enormous datasets in a fraction of the time it would take human researchers is leading to breakthroughs that were previously unimaginable.

For example, companies like Insilico Medicine are using GAI to identify novel drug candidates by analyzing vast molecular datasets. In one notable instance, AI models predicted new compounds for fibrosis treatment in just weeks, significantly shortening the typical drug discovery timeline. This use of GAI is revolutionizing the pharmaceutical industry by reducing both the time and cost of developing new treatments.

Furthermore, AI-generated insights are helping tailor medical treatments to individual patients, enhancing the field of personalized medicine. By analyzing genomic data, lifestyle factors, and medical histories, GAI models can recommend individualized treatment plans that optimize patient outcomes. This represents a major shift from the traditional "one-size-fits-all" approach to treatment.

Challenges and Roadblocks to Large-Scale Adoption

As we touched on in the introduction, while the potential of GAI in healthcare is immense, several hurdles remain before it can be fully integrated into medical practice and research. Let's take a deeper dive into the challenges that AI developers and the healthcare industry still face before all the promises of GAI can become a daily reality.

If you had asked us a year ago what the greatest challenge to Gen AI implementation in healthcare was, we would have said something like "acceptance."

That is no longer the issue. In fact, what we hear from clients all the time is that they "are sold on Gen AI, but we have security and interpretability concerns when using a commercial-off-the-shelf (COTS) solution."

Crystal Broj, with Medical University of South Carolina (MUSC), expressed this very concern to us during our interview.

> One of our biggest challenges is integration with existing systems. Our IT teams are already stretched thin, and connecting new AI tools to legacy infrastructure adds even more work. Many GenAI solutions are still point solutions, which makes it difficult for health systems to scale sustainably — we simply can't support a separate platform for every use case. That's why at Medical University of South Carolina, we're looking for partners, not vendors — those who can grow with us and offer platform-level capabilities across multiple needs.

This is definitely one of the major challenges we face now. As Crystal articulated, even if you go into a customized solution instead of something COTS like MS Copilot, then you have the issue of reliance on an outside vendor. Right now, most healthcare providers rely on third-party vendors to develop and maintain AI systems. This dependency can create vulnerabilities, such as reliance on proprietary systems and a lack of control over data. This is why there is now a growing need and opportunit***ies*** for a Chief AI Officer (CAIO).

Acting as the organization's AI technology expert, the CAIO identifies, evaluates, and implements AI tools and platforms that align with business objectives. They establish best practices for AI development and deployment to maximize efficiency, scalability, and value. Beyond that, the CAIO plays a vital role in shaping the company's corporate culture toward AI by fostering understanding and trust in AI technologies across the organization. They articulate the company's AI strategy both internally, through training and communication, and externally, serving as the public face and advocate of the company's AI vision in industry forums and client engagements.

Another significant challenge facing the adoption of LLMs and GAI in healthcare is the issue of "hallucinations," which is when GAI models generate incorrect or nonsensical information. These kinds of inaccuracies can be an issue in any business, but they are particularly dangerous in a medical context, where precision is critical. Despite their impressive capabilities, LLMs are still prone to generating misleading or incorrect information, particularly when working with ambiguous or incomplete data. This poses a significant risk in medical diagnostics and treatment planning, where errors could have life-threatening consequences.

Similarly, GAI models can perpetuate or even amplify biases present in their training data. For example, datasets that underrepresent certain demographic groups can lead to disparities in healthcare outcomes, undermining the principle of equitable care.

Ethics is another concern; while automation can enhance efficiency, it also raises ethical concerns about replacing human judgment with machine recommendations. Balancing the roles of AI and human expertise is critical to maintaining trust and ethical standards in patient care. The use of GAI in healthcare also introduces new challenges in obtaining informed consent from patients. Explaining how AI models work and how patient data will be used is complex, and many patients may struggle to understand these concepts fully.

Finally, the use of GAI in healthcare also raises complex regulatory challenges. Medical AI tools must comply with stringent regulatory standards set by authorities like the FDA and EMA, particularly around safety, efficacy, and data privacy. The process of getting regulatory approval for AI-driven medical devices is lengthy and complex, often requiring rigorous testing and validation. Additionally, existing regulatory frameworks were not designed with GAI in mind, which has led to uncertainty about how these technologies should be governed. Yet a regulatory framework is absolutely necessary.

Ritu and I are developers and facilitators. We have heard the argument many times about how regulation can stifle innovation and creativity. However, in the case of Gen AI, we share the belief in its necessity. Think of how it was when automobiles were first introduced and became widely available. The government soon recognized that these powerful machines could not be driven willy nilly all over the place without roads being built and rules being put in place. Because of roads, licensing requirements, and traffic laws, millions of miles of superhighways work all over the world. Has that stifled innovation in the automotive industry? Compare a 1910 Model T Ford with a 2025 Tesla Cybertruck, and you tell me!

A similar system and infrastructure, once in place, will only help accelerate acceptance, implementation, and innovation in GAI!

Now that we understand more about the transition from legacy AI to Gen AI for healthcare let's take a deeper dive and look at some of the successful applications currently in use.

Chapter 2

Current Landscape of GAI in Healthcare

[Firstly], GPT-4 is a tool that people have a great deal of control over how they use it. And second, GPT-4 and other systems like it are good at doing tasks, not jobs.

Sam Altman

Generative AI (GAI) is rapidly becoming one of the most transformative technologies in healthcare, with applications spanning diagnostics, drug discovery, administrative efficiencies, and patient care. From radiology and pathology to pharmaceutical innovation, GAI is not just a concept of the future but a vital tool that is reshaping healthcare today.

Now that it is in real-world usage, we are finding the right lane for GAI applications, which is not replacing human interaction but enhancing it. Despite our early fears, to the contrary, the most practical solutions are focused on augmenting rather than automating. As we delve into the successful use cases in this chapter, you will see that humans are still in the loop and very much a part of the picture.

However, while we are already seeing inroads being made in diagnostics, particularly in medical imaging, most of the challenges we discussed at the end of the last chapter, in terms of privacy, hallucinations, etc., are still holding back GAI from reaching its full potential in clinical areas.

Rather, the game-changing solutions are happening less in the clinical setting and more in the administrative setting. For example, automating doctors' notes, generating patient care plans, or reducing the administrative burden. Aashima

DOI: 10.4324/9781003665434-2

Gupta, who serves as the Global Leader of Healthcare Industry Solutions at Google Cloud, has said that the ideal goal of GAI is to allow doctors to do what they are trained to do. She said that these are professionals who have spent their lives training to be diagnostic detectives and to take better care of patients. She says that tech leaders like Google need to focus on developing GAI solutions that reduce the administrative burdens on practitioners so they can concentrate on doing what they've spent all those years training for.

She is not alone in those thoughts. The most successful solutions that are now in play clearly show that the industry has reached that consensus right now. Even though there are GAI solutions that are making a difference in diagnostics, particularly in imaging, there is still greater interest in reducing the administrative burden so doctors can be better doctors.

As we mentioned in our last chapter, a prime example is ambient listening. Estimates are that it saves physicians an average of five to six minutes per patient. That may not sound like very much; however, when you multiply that by 20 patients a day, 30 days a month, you can see how it starts adding up significantly. Then multiply that by hundreds of physicians in a major hospital system, and suddenly, you are achieving enormous gains in terms of productivity.

At the end of the day, focusing on reducing the paperwork burden on physicians does have the net effect of improving patient care. Not only does it allow doctors to do what they were trained to do and to spend more time with their patients, but it also means more free time at home instead of filling out reports and such. This leads to less doctor burnout and more of them actually enjoying the practice of medicine again, which ultimately helps them do their jobs that much better.

All of this is not to say that Gen AI solutions are not having an impact on direct patient care. In fact, the same thing that makes them so good at easing administrative burdens—their near-perfect ability to understand and react to human language—is also helping significantly with certain clinical tasks.

If you look at it from the perspective of startups that are thriving in this space, then what you will discover is that they have honed in on one thing that LLMs do very well—language. It's right there in the acronym. In our last chapter, we mentioned the introduction of virtual assistants and virtual nurses. A key player in this area is Hippocratic AI. Hippocratic has already tested the virtual assistant it has built with NVIDIA on its Polaris platform by recruiting US-licensed nurses and physicians to perform end-to-end conversational evaluations of the system by posing as patients. The company says that, compared to OpenAI's ChatGPT-4 and LLaMA-2 70B and flesh-and-blood nurses, Polaris outperformed them all in terms of safety benchmarks.

Now, they are talking about taking this to the next level by introducing multilingual capabilities to the platform. This was based on a study they performed that found that regardless of what kind of metric they were surveying for, they got nearly three times the level of engagement when they engaged with the test population in their native language. That study was done in Spanish, but now they are creating virtual assistants that can engage in Vietnamese, Creole, Hindi, or any language in a given population, thus creating a pool of multilingual virtual nurses.

Similarly, we worked with a startup known as Mila Health, which deployed an LLM-driven solution to remind patients of necessary follow-up care, appointment reminders, or pre-procedure preparation. For example, if you have a blood test coming up, you can get a notification in your native language that says, "Don't forget to fast for 12 hours before your appointment." This avoids appointments that have to be rescheduled when patients show up and say, "No one told me that," as often happens with non-English speaking patients.

Another very interesting case where the power of LLMs to use and interpret human language led to improved patient care was a VA hospital system that used the solution of a successful AI startup known as Narratize. According to the company Narratize, it is an "AI-powered storytelling platform that drives innovation success by transforming scientific, technical, and medical insights into compelling stories, fast."

In this case, the nurses used the application to let veterans in the hospitals craft their stories. When the nurses who were caring for those patients read those stories, it really humanized the veterans for them. The nursing staff became much more empathetic to the patients because, after reading the stories created by the AI—each patient's personal "narrative," if you will—they saw the patient not as a number or just a body in a bed but a real human being with real backstory.

When the departments involved tracked the outcomes of the patients involved in the storytelling, they found that those patients had better recovery rates than those not involved in the experiment because the nurses became more loving and more empathetic to these men and women who had served and sacrificed.

These results echoed those of a project that was initiated in 2015 called "My Life, My Story," which was instituted at the William S. Middleton Memorial Veterans Hospital in Madison, Wisconsin. The results of that program, published in *The Federal Practitioner*, found that allowing Vets to share their personal narratives "reduced anger, depression, tension, and an increased sense of peace and have shown to reduce psychological distress, increase hope, and help the patient feel valued." The analysis of this and similar efforts also found that this kind of storytelling helps bridge the gap between veterans and civilians, fostering greater empathy, understanding, and support.

However, these early efforts all relied on the tedious process of staff or volunteers interviewing the veterans, taking notes on their stories, and then using their own skills and talents to craft compelling stories out of them—something that Narratize does in practically no time!

In addition to clinical and administrative tasks, another domain in healthcare that is currently witnessing significant transformation through GAI is drug discovery. Traditionally, the drug discovery pipeline is lengthy and expensive, often taking upwards of a decade and costing billions of dollars to bring a new drug to market. GAI accelerates this process by simulating molecular interactions, predicting the efficacy of compounds, and optimizing chemical structures. This reduces the need for physical experimentation, which can take years, and allows researchers to focus on the most promising drug candidates.

Let's take a look at some other specific cases of successful use of LLM and GAI technology across a wide spectrum of healthcare interests and stakeholders.

Medical Imaging

One of the most notable examples of GAI in medical imaging comes from Google Health. In 2020, Google Health developed an AI model capable of outperforming radiologists in detecting breast cancer through mammography. In a peer-reviewed study, the model reduced false negatives by 9.4% and false positives by 5.7%, which could translate to thousands of lives saved through earlier detection. Zebra Medical Vision, another major player, has developed AI tools that analyze X-rays to detect conditions like osteoporosis and cardiovascular diseases, improving early diagnosis and patient outcomes.

Aidoc's AI-powered imaging solutions can flag life-threatening conditions such as intracranial hemorrhages and pulmonary embolisms in real-time, enabling radiologists to prioritize urgent cases. This capability significantly reduces diagnostic turnaround times, which is critical for emergency care.

Additionally, GAI models are being integrated into ultrasound technology, where they assist in prenatal screenings by detecting abnormalities in fetal development. By providing real-time analysis and highlighting potential issues, these tools enhance the accuracy of prenatal care and ensure that complications are identified early.

Operational Efficiency and Knowledge Management

The Mayo Clinic has adopted AI to streamline administrative tasks such as patient scheduling, medical documentation, and resource management. By automating these processes, the clinic has reduced administrative overhead by 30%, allowing healthcare providers to focus more on patient care. This operational efficiency has resulted in higher patient satisfaction rates and improved healthcare outcomes.

While not a name usually associated with the healthcare industry, Nestlé's experience with Gen AI bears mentioning. In 2024, the world-renowned chocolate maker released NesGPT. It is a proprietary internal GAI solution specifically designed to boost the efficiency of its corporate workforce. According to the company, the tool is used across various business functions, including sales, product innovation, marketing, and legal teams. This includes using the tool for support in drafting content, drafting meeting agendas, proofreading, generating new ideas, analyzing data, and explaining new topics or concepts.

After one year of use, the company reported that it's saving Nestlé employees, on average, 45 minutes of work time each week, primarily creating better and faster content and spending less time searching for information.

"What's really exciting is that gen AI technology has progressed significantly in a short period of time," said Shan Collins, head of IT North America, Nestlé. "That, combined with our employees getting early experience in how to leverage these solutions as a digital personal assistant, will open up more opportunities and generate even greater benefits for our employees and the business."

Imagine being able to use AI to take the entire knowledge database of your company, all the disparate information from notes to White Papers to emails and meeting transcripts, and put them into one repository, easily searchable just by asking a virtual assistant. That is exactly what multinational business consulting firm McKinsey and Company has done with the creation of "Lilli," their Siri-like virtual researcher. According to the company, it provides a streamlined, impartial search and synthesis of the firm's vast stores of knowledge to bring our best insights quickly and efficiently to clients.

"Lilli aggregates our knowledge and capabilities in one place for the first time and will allow us to spend more time with clients activating those insights and recommendations and maximizing the value we can create," says Erik Roth, a senior partner with McKinsey who leads the firm's development of Lilli. "An engagement team will be able to spend more time on problem-solving, coaching, building capabilities, and helping clients achieve the performance they aspire to achieve."

Lilli, which the firm says was named after the company's first female employee, can access and leverage McKinsey's entire body of knowledge and assets. Now, any analyst can simply ask Lilli a question, and "she" brings back all the summarized and collated data into one place, driving new levels of productivity. Roth points out that one of the things that makes Lilli so exciting is that it not only can search the company's entire body of knowledge in response to a client's query, but it can find answers or relevant data in places human researchers would not think to look because it can find patterns and connections in the unconstructed data that humans cannot.

Lilli, while not specifically designed or used in healthcare, is a dramatic example of what we try to teach people about Gen AI in our workshops. One of the major differences between Gen AI and other forms of machine learning that have come before is that Gen AI is not only capable of doing things more efficiently, but it's also about doing things in a completely different way. If legacy AI can think, then Gen AI can "think out of the box."

Expanding Patient Engagement and Remote Monitoring

Beyond diagnostics, drug discovery, and productivity enhancement, GAI enriches patient engagement through personalized health monitoring and remote patient management. Wearable devices equipped with AI algorithms monitor vital signs and detect anomalies in real time, alerting patients and healthcare providers to potential health issues before they escalate. This continuous monitoring allows for early intervention, reducing hospital admissions and improving long-term health outcomes.

An example of this technology is Biofourmis, a company that uses AI to monitor patients with chronic conditions remotely. Biofourmis' platform analyzes data from wearable devices, predicting adverse health events and enabling proactive intervention by healthcare teams. This reduces the risk of hospitalization and improves patient quality of life.

Customer Relationship Management

Customer relationship management, or "CRM," is another non-clinical area where GAI is making a transformative difference in healthcare. CRM is the combination of practices, strategies, and technologies that companies use to manage and analyze customer interactions and data throughout the customer lifecycle. GAI can be integrated into CRM systems to automate routine tasks, assist with data analysis, and enhance customer interactions. This can vastly improve the healthcare industry, which is plagued by complaints of poor customer service.

A constant criticism among healthcare consumers is "feeling like a number" and dealing with hospitals and healthcare providers that seem to lack a personal touch in a setting where that should be the rule rather than the exception.

GAI is changing all that with its unique ability to craft deeply individualized customer exchanges. Drawing from past data, CRMs infused with GAI can create bespoke emails and responses, bypassing the old "one-size-fits-all" approach. In tandem with this, the technology's predictive prowess can foresee a patient's future needs, desires, and actions. This foresight lets customer care agents jump in with solutions or offerings, often before the client even voices their requirements.

Salesforce is a recognized leader in CRM. The latest offering from Salesforce, Salesforce Einstein, leverages GAI to enhance CRM capabilities. It offers predictive lead scoring, automated email responses, and dynamic pricing recommendations. Leading healthcare organizations like Sentara Healthcare are utilizing Salesforce for marketing automation, patient/member engagement, creating patient 360s, and online scheduling.

Drug Discovery

Insilco Medicine made headlines by using AI to identify a novel drug candidate for idiopathic pulmonary fibrosis in less than 18 months, a process that typically takes 4–5 years. Insilico's platform used GAI to generate and test thousands of molecular structures, selecting the most promising candidates for laboratory testing. Atomwise, another leader in AI-driven drug discovery, uses convolutional neural networks to predict how drugs interact with target proteins, significantly accelerating drug screening processes. Atomwise's technology has been used to identify potential treatments for diseases such as Ebola and multiple sclerosis.

The application of GAI in drug discovery is particularly revolutionary. One of the key advantages of GAI is its ability to analyze vast datasets of chemical structures and biological information to identify potential drug candidates. Companies like BenevolentAI and Recursion Pharmaceuticals use AI to sift through millions of data points, uncovering relationships that would otherwise go unnoticed.

BenevolentAI's platform was instrumental in identifying a promising drug candidate for COVID-19 by repurposing an existing arthritis medication. This rapid identification and repurposing process demonstrated how GAI could respond to urgent global health crises by accelerating the development of treatments.

Furthermore, AI-driven platforms can predict the likelihood of drug toxicity, reducing the risk of failure in clinical trials. This predictive capability is crucial for reducing the attrition rate in pharmaceutical research and development, ultimately lowering the overall cost of bringing new drugs to market.

We will take a much deeper dive into GAI applications for drug discovery and medical research in Chapter 9.

What Do They All Have in Common?

If we dissect all of the real-world examples and case studies discussed above, does a pattern emerge? What do they all have in common? What makes for a successful implementation of GAI in the healthcare arena?

The first commonality you will find in each of these examples is that they started with a company that had an appetite for experimentation and a willingness to take a risk and put dollars behind it. They knew that the return on their investment was not a given, but they were willing to plunge headlong into the future. It's like the difference between NASA and space entrepreneurs like SpaceX; NASA's motto was "failure is not an option." But for SpaceX, when their rocket blows up three minutes mid-flight, they don't consider that a failure but a *success* because that is three minutes of new data they did not have before.

As counterintuitive as it may sound, successful implementation of GAI in healthcare has to start with a willingness to fail. All of the examples cited above were deployed by companies willing to experiment and possibly fail, but who understood that success is built upon what can be learned from failure.

While a willingness to experiment and potentially fail is a common beginning, successful early adopters also do not start from scratch. They all already had, if not legacy AI solutions to build off of, at least an IT infrastructure in place. The amount of people and resources needed to build and train a successful LLM-driven GAI model would be far too costly to start without a team of developers, engineers, product managers, and the support of C-level execs who already have a track record of successful tech rollouts. If you look closely at the use cases mentioned in this chapter, you will find that this was true of them all.

What's Next?

The healthcare industry is a complex and data-rich field that requires constant innovation to improve patient care, enhance diagnostic accuracy, and streamline administrative processes. Looking ahead, the role of GAI in healthcare will continue to expand as more institutions adopt and integrate these technologies.

As new GAI solutions are introduced, they will continue to improve efficiency and productivity across the many moving parts of the healthcare system. Innovative startups will focus on specific components, such as accelerating clinical trials or improving diagnostics and disease detection. This will have a ripple effect on the healthcare industry as a whole, making it less expensive to run and, at the same time, more customer-centric.

Let's gaze deeper into this crystal ball in Chapter 3.

Chapter 3

Future Directions and Innovations

Generative models are a key enabler of machine creativity, allowing machines to go beyond what they've seen before and create something new.

Ian Goodfellow

Over the course of our exploration in the first two chapters, we established how generative AI (GAI) tools are already changing the healthcare landscape, ushering in novel capabilities for diagnostics, patient engagement, medical documentation, and more. We have seen how the synergy between technology and medicine is propelling the field forward at a rate that few industries can match. In Chapter 3, we turn our gaze toward the future, focusing on the potential directions and innovations that GAI may bring to healthcare in the years to come. We will look at emerging trends and explore how they might reshape patient care, clinical workflows, research, and therapeutic interventions. While many of these ideas are grounded in existing research and trends, some remain speculative, yet nonetheless provide a glimpse into the remarkable transformations that might lie ahead.

"When it comes to healthcare, in the US, it is generally recognized that (1) costs are too high and (2) outcomes could be much better. I contend that AI will materially help with both," said Vinod Khosla, entrepreneur, investor, technologist, and founder of Khosla Ventures.

> In the very short term, AI will provide us with nearly free expertise at the rapidly declining cost of computation in outpatient care. AI conversations can engage, diagnose, and monitor patients, all

DOI: 10.4324/9781003665434-3

> while understanding their issues. Applying advanced diagnostic reasoning, a deep understanding of the latest medical research, and superior analysis of interactions between conditions, events, lifestyles, and social determinants is now economically feasible, thanks to GAI.

As Mr. Khosla says, there is broad potential for Gen-AI to create an entirely new healthcare landscape where we will see things like personalized medicine, revolutionary drug discovery, advanced training for healthcare professionals, robotic surgeries, integration with IoT, and more, all leading to a more patient-centric care model. However, long before any of this happens, there will be a shakeout where things will start to consolidate, especially from a startup perspective. There will be certain startups with much more narrow or targeted applications that will bust out and take a wide lead over the others, with innovative use cases for large language models (LLMs) leading the pack. The most successful of these technologies will become commonplace and set the standard for the "must-haves" of GAI for healthcare, which is exactly how ambient listening is doing right now. As the industry starts to unite around certain technologies, adoption will accelerate.

Once the healthcare industry achieves that level of comfort with ambient listening and LLM tools overall, we feel the next "must-have" technology will be voice agents and multi-agent systems (MASs). These are at the introductory level of the curve right now, but will be essential to the fundamental paradigm shift that will provide the picture of the future of GAI we are painting in this chapter.

What Are Multi-Agent Systems and How Will They Contribute to the Healthcare GAI Future

A MAS is a group of AI agents that work together to complete tasks. MASs are a key area of AI research. In a MAS, multiple, relatively autonomous agents—each with its own objectives, capabilities, and decision-making processes—coexist and interact within a shared environment. These agents can be designed to collaborate, compete, or use a combination of both strategies to achieve individual or collective goals. In contrast to a single GAI model tackling a problem, MASs distribute the computational tasks among diverse specialized agents, which can yield richer insights and more dynamic problem-solving behaviors.

When applied to GAI, multi-agent architectures can enhance performance, robustness, and creativity in several ways. Different agents can be specialized to handle specific subtasks, such as data preprocessing, model training, outcome verification, and bias detection. By delegating tasks, each agent can capitalize on its strengths (e.g., natural language generation, image synthesis, or interpretability algorithms), yielding higher-quality outputs overall.

MASs have the potential to dramatically reshape healthcare by introducing sophisticated, collaborative intelligence into clinical and operational workflows. For example, in complex clinical scenarios, such as intensive care units, a MAS might include specialized agents for real-time patient monitoring, predictive modeling, and treatment recommendations. Each agent focuses on a different data stream (vitals, labs, imaging, etc.), collectively providing clinicians with an integrated view and actionable suggestions. Looking at healthcare setting from a broader view in a MAS, one agent might generate a synthetic patient dataset; a second agent could assess its fidelity or ethical compliance; a third agent could suggest modifications to minimize bias or improve representativeness. Over successive interactions, the final result is a more thoroughly vetted and polished GAI output.

In their landmark article, *Coordinated AI Agents for Advancing healthcare,* published in Nature Biomedical Engineering, Michael Moritz, Eric Topol, and Pranav Rajpurkar paint a hopeful and technically grounded picture of what's possible when AI systems stop working in isolation and start working together. They conclude that MASs "[are] not about replacing doctors, it's about giving them a team of tireless, brilliant assistants who make healthcare better for everyone."

As we begin our discussion of the potential advancements of healthcare-GAI, it is MAS's that will bring us to the first one on our list—personalized medicine. With multi-agent orchestration, generative models can synthesize a patient's genetic, lifestyle, and environmental data to propose tailored treatments. Other agents in the system can simulate likely outcomes, run safety checks, or cross-reference the latest clinical guidelines, effectively acting as a built-in second opinion for clinicians.

Potential Advancements in GAI and Their Implications

Predictive Modeling for Personalized Medicine

Predictive modeling in medicine involves using advanced statistical techniques and machine learning algorithms to forecast health outcomes for individual patients or populations. By harnessing the wealth of biomedical data—from electronic health records (EHRs) to genomic information—GAI systems can identify patterns that human analysts might miss. In the very near future, GAI could generate robust predictive models that not only identify these patterns but also formulate targeted interventions, potentially revolutionizing personalized medicine.

Thus far, AI-driven predictive modeling in healthcare has largely revolved around conventional machine learning and deep learning approaches. Examples include algorithms that predict hospital readmissions, forecast the progression of chronic diseases like diabetes, or analyze tumor growth in oncology. For instance, the company Tempus has been working on integrating clinical data, pathology images, and genomic data to provide oncologists with data-driven insights. While these systems have shown promise, they still require complex data preprocessing, feature engineering, and manual oversight.

With GAI, there is the potential to automate or semi-automate many of these preprocessing tasks. Tools like LLMs could be trained on vast corpora of both structured and unstructured medical data, generating synthetic patient histories, refining data labeling, and providing more holistic patient profiles that can then be fed into predictive models. This might enable healthcare providers to proactively intervene well before a crisis, such as a stroke, heart attack, or other acute event, materializes.

As GAI systems become more advanced, they will likely integrate seamlessly with health data from a wide variety of sources—genomics, proteomics, metabolomics, imaging, lifestyle metrics, and more. The result could be hyper-personalized health risk assessments and prevention plans. Imagine a scenario in which a generative model factors in an individual's genetic predispositions, dietary patterns, living environment, and psychological status to predict not only the likelihood of developing a specific disease but also the exact moment the risk becomes critical. It might then suggest a personalized "health maintenance plan," replete with dietary suggestions, exercise guidelines, mental health breaks, and pharmaceutical interventions if needed.

These predictive models also open up the possibility of real-time monitoring and ongoing risk stratification. If integrated into wearable devices (which we will discuss in more detail later), a GAI system could detect subtle fluctuations in vital signs that indicate deteriorating health. By flagging these changes proactively, these systems might help patients avoid hospitalization altogether or ensure that medical interventions are delivered much earlier than would be possible under traditional care models.

Looking further ahead, there is a strong possibility that GAI-enabled systems will be able to produce therapeutics tailored to an individual's unique genetic or molecular profile. This might include custom cell therapies or precision medications designed specifically to counter genetic mutations found in a patient's tumor cells. Advances in mRNA technology, as shown by Moderna and BioNTech during the COVID-19 pandemic, hint at what might be achievable once we add GAI's capability to design personalized sequences with high specificity and efficacy.

While the potential benefits are vast, there are still hurdles. Regulatory pathways for AI-discovered drugs will need to be refined to ensure safety. Furthermore, the molecular complexity of certain diseases could outstrip even advanced AI modeling capabilities if the underlying biological mechanisms are not well understood. Still, the direction is clear: GAI could substantially compress drug discovery timelines and costs, while simultaneously unlocking novel therapeutic frontiers.

Revolutionizing Drug Discovery and Pharma Research

Drug discovery is notoriously time-consuming and expensive. On average, bringing a new drug to market can cost billions of dollars and take over a decade. GAI holds the potential to reshape this process by automating many of the steps involved in identifying viable drug candidates, optimizing molecules, and even designing novel compounds.

Traditional computational drug discovery often starts with large-scale screening of compound libraries—a process that can be enhanced by machine learning. GAI goes a step further by proposing entirely new molecular structures that meet specified criteria for potency, bioavailability, and safety. Companies like Insilico Medicine and BenevolentAI have already demonstrated the power of using AI-generated compound designs, reducing the lead time for identifying potential drug candidates from years to months or even weeks.

Beyond discovering entirely new molecules, GAI could also be used for optimizing existing medications. By analyzing complex datasets, these systems could reveal unknown off-target effects or potential drug-drug interactions. This can be particularly beneficial for elderly patients, who often take multiple medications simultaneously.

Another key area where GAI can shine is in drug repositioning—identifying new therapeutic uses for existing medications. For instance, a widely known success story is the repositioning of the drug sildenafil (originally researched for hypertension) for erectile dysfunction, which led to the blockbuster brand Viagra. In the future, GAI tools might systematically screen existing molecular libraries and propose new therapeutic targets, thus accelerating the repositioning process and saving considerable time and resources.

Synthetic Data Generation for Healthcare Research and Training

Why Synthetic Data?

High-quality clinical data is the lifeblood of medical research and innovation. However, patient privacy regulations like HIPAA (in the US) and GDPR (in the EU) significantly constrain the sharing of sensitive healthcare data. This is where GAI can play a transformative role: by producing synthetic datasets that mirror the statistical properties of real patient data without revealing personal identifiers, GAI systems can circumvent many privacy concerns.

For instance, a hospital might wish to collaborate with a pharmaceutical company to study the real-world performance of a specific cancer therapy across thousands of patient records. Traditional data-sharing agreements can be cumbersome, with extensive de-identification processes that risk losing valuable information. Using generative models—such as variational autoencoders (VAEs) or generative adversarial networks (GANs)—the hospital could generate a synthetic dataset that closely resembles the real dataset in terms of clinical features, disease progression, and treatment outcomes. The pharmaceutical company can then use this synthetic dataset to develop or refine its predictive models, all without accessing actual patient data.

Applications in Medical Training and Simulation

Synthetic data has implications well beyond research collaborations. In medical training, AI-generated patient scenarios can expose medical students and resident physicians to a wider range of cases than they might otherwise encounter. For example, generative models could create realistic radiology images that present rare pathologies, allowing trainees to hone their diagnostic skills. At the same time, these trainees could practice "virtual consults" with GAI chatbots simulating patient interviews, fine-tuning their communication and clinical reasoning in a risk-free environment.

Similarly, synthetic data can power advanced simulations of surgical procedures, emergency scenarios, or epidemic outbreaks. Imagine an entire simulated pandemic scenario where health leaders can test various interventions, logistical strategies, and resource allocation plans—all without actual human lives at stake. While such large-scale simulations already exist, GAI can make them exponentially more detailed and adaptable, ensuring that the training is as close to reality as possible.

Ethical and Regulatory Considerations

A major advantage of synthetic data is the reduced risk of violating patient confidentiality. However, there are still concerns regarding data fidelity. If generative models inadvertently incorporate artifacts or biases from the real dataset, they might perpetuate existing inequities or introduce flawed patterns. Regulators and healthcare institutions will need robust validation protocols to ensure that synthetic data is both accurate and representative.

Another dimension to consider is the ownership and intellectual property rights of synthetic data. If a generative model trained on a hospital's data produces a synthetic dataset, to what extent does the hospital maintain rights over it? Will external collaborators, such as pharmaceutical companies or AI startups, also claim partial ownership? These are pressing questions that the healthcare industry will need to address as the adoption of synthetic data generation grows.

How Far Can We Go? Additional Cutting-Edge Directions

While predictive modeling, drug design, and synthetic data generation are among the most prominent potential applications of GAI in healthcare, several other areas hold immense promise:

1. **Telehealth and Virtual Care Assistants**: Voice-enabled generative agents could serve as first-line triage tools, offering patients immediate advice, appointment scheduling, and routing to the correct healthcare specialist. These agents might also support chronic disease management by reminding patients to take medications or complete routine tests.
2. **Generative AI for Surgical and Procedural Training**: By merging generative models with augmented reality (AR) or virtual reality (VR) platforms, medical professionals can receive highly detailed, real-time surgical simulations. AI-driven adjustments in these simulations can match the trainee's skill level, providing immediate feedback and iterative skill-building opportunities.
3. **Prosthetics and Orthotics**: Generative design tools could be used to quickly develop customized prosthetic limbs or orthopedic supports that consider a patient's unique anatomy and biomechanics. Companies like Unlimited Tomorrow are already using 3D scanning and AI to create personalized prosthetics, and generative design could streamline the process even more.

4. **GAI-Enhanced Robotics**: Robots equipped with generative models could learn and adapt more dynamically, providing assistance in tasks like disinfecting patient wards, delivering medical supplies, or even helping in surgical procedures. For instance, a GAI-enabled robotic surgical assistant might "learn" from previous surgeries and adapt to unexpected conditions better than a purely rule-based system.
5. **GAI for Mental Health**: Mental health services could benefit from AI-driven therapy bots that simulate different therapeutic approaches or dialectical behavior therapy (DBT) scenarios. While human therapists will remain crucial, GAI could relieve some of the strain on overburdened mental healthcare systems and provide immediate support to patients who might otherwise face long waiting lists.
6. **Disease Detection: Identification of Rare or Unusual Symptoms**: Medical "detective work" or what doctors refer to as a "differential diagnosis"—trying to figure out what is going on from a set of symptoms—can be greatly advanced by GAI. For example, Epic Systems Corporation, the industry standard for EMR software, has recently introduced something known as Epic Cosmos. It is a dataset curated by Epic that is made up of an anonymous record—symptoms and diagnosis only, no ID info about the patient - in the Epic database. A physician at any practice, clinic, or medical center using Epic, which is thousands, can look into those records and cross-reference a patient with unusual symptoms that they may be having trouble diagnosing. He can use the system to see if there's a physician anywhere in the US who has had a similar patient almost instantly. He can then get in touch with that physician and find out how he treated this patient, which is quite remarkable!

From Assistant to Autonomous System?

Perhaps one of the most intriguing questions is whether GAI might transition from being a powerful but ultimately supervised assistant to an autonomous agent capable of making independent clinical decisions. While many experts caution against granting AI full autonomy, citing ethical, legal, and reliability concerns, there are scenarios where near-autonomous GAI systems might be beneficial. For example:

- **Radiology and Pathology**: Automated image analysis tools that diagnose and categorize conditions like cancer might eventually become so accurate that human oversight is minimal, reserved only for particularly complex or ambiguous cases.

- **Medication Management**: AI systems that monitor patients' daily medication intake, watch for signs of adverse reactions, and adjust dosages could theoretically operate with minimal human intervention, especially in low-risk scenarios.
- **Rural and Underserved Areas**: In remote regions with a scarcity of healthcare professionals, near-autonomous AI-driven diagnostic kiosks or mobile units might provide essential medical services, bridging significant gaps in care.

While such prospects are compelling, the journey to full autonomy is far from straightforward. Issues like bias in AI training data, interpretability of complex models, and the "black box" nature of deep learning-based systems are significant challenges that must be addressed before mainstream healthcare entrusts AI with fully autonomous tasks.

Expansion into Global Health

GAI also holds the promise of revolutionizing healthcare in low-resource settings. By lowering the costs of diagnostic tools (for example, generating cheaper molecular diagnostics or simplified imaging techniques), GAI could extend advanced care to areas where the healthcare infrastructure is less developed. It can also facilitate translation services for remote telemedicine consults, bridging language barriers. Mobile phone-based GAI tools can guide community health workers through complex procedures or diagnoses, effectively democratizing access to medical expertise.

Integration with Wearable Devices and the Internet of Things

A New Frontier in Continuous Monitoring

Wearable devices—ranging from smartwatches to patches that monitor vital signs—are rapidly proliferating. Many consumers now routinely track their heart rate, sleep patterns, and activity levels. GAI can supercharge this trend by intelligently synthesizing data from a multitude of personal devices, creating a comprehensive health profile that can be monitored in real-time.

In an everyday scenario, an individual's smartwatch might detect irregular heartbeats, while a glucose monitors alerts to slight elevations in blood sugar. Simultaneously, a smart scale at home records changes in body composition, and a smart ring tracks sleep quality. By aggregating all this data, a GAI system can generate predictive insights about the user's cardiovascular risk profile, metabolic health, and potential for sleep disorders. It can even "speak" with other IoT-enabled devices, such as the user's smart refrigerator or treadmill, to make personalized suggestions, like adjusting temperature or providing workout recommendations based on fatigue levels.

Medical-Grade Wearables and Clinical-Grade Insights

While consumer wearables provide useful general insights, the next wave of devices will likely be specifically engineered for medical settings. For instance, continuous ECG monitors, blood pressure sensors, and even small ultrasound probes could feed high-fidelity data directly into GAI-driven platforms. Hospitals and clinics might issue these devices to patients upon discharge, enabling practitioners to monitor them remotely, anticipate complications, and intervene swiftly when needed.

Imagine a patient who has just undergone open-heart surgery being sent home with a suite of wireless sensors. These sensors track everything from daily activity levels to subtle changes in oxygen saturation. A GAI platform would generate dynamic recovery roadmaps, adjusting rehabilitation exercises, alerting healthcare providers to warning signs (like fluid build-up), and providing the patient with motivational messaging. This kind of "closed-loop" care system could significantly reduce readmissions and complications.

Data Privacy and Security

The integration of wearables and IoT devices with GAI raises critical concerns around data security. Unlike traditional EHR data, stored in relatively controlled hospital systems, wearable data flows across a vast ecosystem of devices, apps, and cloud services. Cybersecurity protocols must evolve to safeguard this data, ensuring that malicious actors cannot exploit vulnerabilities. Additionally, new regulations may be required to clarify how consumer-generated health data should be protected, who owns it, and how it may be used for research or commercial purposes.

Empowering Patients for Better Outcomes: The Shift to a Patient-Centric Care Model

One of the most transformative aspects of GAI in healthcare is the potential to shift from provider-centric to patient-centric care. In a patient-centric model, the individual is an active participant, rather than a passive recipient, of healthcare services. GAI tools can help by providing patients with easy-to-understand insights, personalized educational materials, and 24/7 access to virtual support.

For instance, after a new diagnosis (say, Type 2 diabetes), a patient might use a GAI-enabled application to learn more about the condition, set diet and exercise goals, and get personalized coaching. The AI assistant could generate meal plans aligned with the patient's cultural and dietary preferences, track adherence through wearable integration, and even predict possible complications or mood fluctuations. This kind of proactive engagement can significantly improve self-management, reduce hospital visits, and empower individuals to take charge of their health.

David H. Berger, MD, MHCM told us, "When I think about the different places where artificial intelligence could have a major impact, I break it down really into four different areas. The first one is obviously back-office functions—things like revenue cycle, coding, billing, documentation, pre-authorization. All those things that have to do with revenue cycle."

Dr. Berger continued, "Then I look at the front end or access—giving patients the opportunity to interact with a provider, giving them the opportunity to schedule, how they're going to pay for their healthcare, et cetera. and then on the care delivery side, there are things that help make care easier to deliver. When I say make it easier to deliver care, I'm talking about things like artificial intelligence scribes or ambient listening.

When I talk about things that help actually *deliver* care, I'm looking at adjuncts to help read X-rays and other scans. For example, radiologists often have difficulty quantitating breast density, and there can be a lack of correlation from one radiologist to another. But using artificial intelligence, you can improve the ability to determine breast density to almost 95 percent accuracy."

Dr. Berger is a digital health entrepreneur and former Chief Executive Officer of University Hospital at Downstate. He also served as the Senior Vice President and Chief Operating Officer of Baylor St. Luke's Medical Center in Houston.

Real-World Examples of Patient Empowerment

Several startups and healthcare systems have begun embracing patient empowerment strategies driven by advanced AI. For example, Ada Health provides an AI-powered symptom checker that helps patients understand potential causes of their symptoms. Meanwhile, platforms like MyFitnessPal and Noom are using data-driven approaches to encourage better nutritional habits. Although these platforms are not all purely generative in their current state, the transition to more sophisticated GAI-based interfaces is likely. Patients might soon engage with chatbots that simulate empathetic human coaches, respond dynamically to unique patient situations, and even generate daily "micro-goals."

This shift to a more patient-centric model of medicine is perhaps the most exciting change that GAI can bring to health delivery. We call the industry "healthcare"; however, the practice of medicine, particularly western medicine, is more "sick-care" than "healthcare." In other words, for centuries, medicine has focused on being reactive—treating a disease after the symptoms present—rather than proactive—preventing diseases before they occur and optimizing health.

The kinds of advances in GAI we have been talking about may finally make healthcare live up to its name!

Health Equity Considerations

As GAI amplifies patient engagement, we must also recognize the risk of exacerbating health disparities. Low-income or elderly populations might not have reliable internet access or the technical proficiency to use advanced apps and wearables. A future dominated by GAI-driven healthcare must incorporate robust accessibility measures, such as simplified user interfaces, multilingual support, and partnerships with community organizations. Additionally, healthcare providers, policy-makers, and industry players must ensure that GAI solutions do not inadvertently embed biases that disadvantage underrepresented groups.

The Sky's The Limit: Other Potential Game-Changing Innovations

Advanced Robotics and Remote Surgery

We have touched on robotics in brief, but the marriage of GAI and robotics in the operating room merits a deeper look. Surgical robots like Intuitive Surgical's da Vinci system are already enabling surgeons to perform minimally invasive procedures with unprecedented precision. As GAI evolves, it could generate real-time surgical guidance, predicting the next best incision point, or even adjusting robotic arms to minimize tissue damage. In remote areas, 5G or satellite-based networks could facilitate tele-robotic surgeries, allowing top surgeons to operate on patients across the globe. GAI could also handle unstructured scenarios that arise mid-surgery, such as unexpected bleeding, by generating instant alternative approaches.

The Rise of Virtual Nursing Assistants

Given the global nursing shortage, especially highlighted by the COVID-19 pandemic, there is a growing interest in leveraging AI to provide routine patient care.

Virtual nursing assistants (VNAs) powered by GAI might be capable of handling preliminary triage, medication reminders, and patient education. They can interpret data from a patient's EHR, wearable devices, or even real-time dialogues to deliver personalized care instructions. These assistants could be accessible through smart speakers or mobile applications, providing near-constant support and guidance to patients, especially those with chronic conditions like heart failure or COPD.

Adaptive Clinical Trials

Clinical trials have historically been rigid: a certain number of participants follow a fixed protocol. GAI could enable adaptive trials that dynamically evolve based on real-time participant data. If an emerging pattern indicates that a subset of patients is responding exceptionally well to a particular dosage, the trial design could shift to concentrate more resources on that dosage group. Conversely, if severe side effects emerge, the GAI system could recommend immediate alterations. This level of responsiveness might reduce both the time and cost of bringing new therapies to market, while also prioritizing patient safety.

AI-Generated Health Education and Awareness Campaigns

Another intriguing avenue for GAI is in public health outreach. By analyzing social media trends, demographic data, and epidemiological patterns, GAI can craft targeted health campaigns—for example, generating localized messaging to encourage vaccinations or screening programs. These campaigns can be delivered in multiple languages and adjusted to resonate with specific cultural nuances. Real-world examples include the use of ChatGPT-like systems to create plain-language summaries of clinical guidelines or new research findings, making crucial health information more digestible for broader audiences.

Can We Get There? Challenges and Considerations for a GAI-Driven Future

Ethical and Legal Dilemmas

- **Bias in Models:** One of the most pressing ethical concerns surrounding AI is bias, be it racial, gender, or socioeconomic. GAI can inadvertently perpetuate biases found in its training data. If these biases inform clinical decisions, they could lead to inequitable care. Rigorous auditing and transparent data sourcing are essential to mitigate this risk.

- **Data Privacy**: As GAI relies on large datasets, patients may worry about who has access to their information. Even synthetic data can pose residual risks if the model is not properly "scrubbed" of potentially identifiable patterns.
- **Accountability**: Who is held accountable when an AI-driven decision leads to a negative outcome? Physicians, hospital administrators, or the AI developers? Clear guidelines must be developed to delineate responsibility.

Regulatory Landscape

Regulatory bodies such as the FDA, EMA, and others around the world are wrestling with how to oversee AI, especially generative models that can produce novel and unpredictable outputs. We may see new frameworks that demand "explainability" or "interpretability" for AI-driven decisions in medicine. These frameworks might require rigorous validation studies comparable to clinical trials, forcing GAI algorithms to demonstrate safety and efficacy before widespread adoption. Such measures are critical to maintain public trust and ensure patient safety.

Acceptance by Medical Professionals

Healthcare professionals may exhibit varying degrees of trust in AI systems, especially when it comes to generative models. Some might embrace these tools as a way to reduce workload and enhance patient care, while others may worry that over-reliance on AI diminishes clinical intuition. Education and transparency are key here. Physicians, nurses, and other clinicians need clear insights into how GAI systems arrive at their recommendations or predictions, as well as opportunities for continued professional development to effectively collaborate with AI-driven technologies.

Infrastructure and Cost

Implementing GAI solutions requires considerable computing power, robust IT infrastructure, and ongoing maintenance. Small clinics and rural hospitals may struggle to afford these investments. Funding models—perhaps through government grants or private-public partnerships—could help level the playing field, ensuring that advanced GAI tools are not limited to well-funded urban centers.

The Path to Mainstream Integration

If we extrapolate the exponential growth in AI capabilities witnessed over the last decade, it becomes plausible that GAI will evolve from a niche tool into a standard component of healthcare infrastructure. One can imagine a future where every major hospital and clinic uses AI-driven systems for tasks ranging from administrative documentation and patient triage to advanced analytics and therapeutic design. This mainstream adoption will be fueled by:

- **Cloud Computing and Edge AI**: With the continued rise of cloud computing platforms (e.g., AWS, Microsoft Azure, Google Cloud) and the proliferation of edge devices capable of running advanced models, healthcare institutions of all sizes may find it feasible to integrate GAI into daily operations.
- **User-Friendly Interfaces**: Currently, many advanced AI tools require specialized data science skills to deploy effectively. However, as user interfaces become more intuitive, healthcare professionals will be able to leverage GAI without necessarily needing deep technical expertise.
- **Evolving Regulatory Frameworks**: Regulatory bodies around the world are gradually developing guidelines for AI in healthcare. We can expect clearer frameworks that define standards, certification processes, and best practices for GAI, thus reducing legal uncertainties.

A Collaborative Vision for Healthcare

Despite the myriad challenges—from ethical quandaries to technological limitations—the potential for GAI to revolutionize healthcare is extraordinary. The trajectory we are on suggests that GAI's role in the field will only become more prominent, interweaving with nearly every aspect of the care continuum.

Collaborative Ecosystems

One key driver of successful GAI integration will be collaboration. Healthcare institutions, technology companies, regulatory agencies, and patient advocacy groups must work in tandem to shape responsible guidelines. This includes shared data repositories, joint research initiatives, and collaborative platforms where best practices are openly discussed. Partnerships like the AI for Health initiative by Microsoft and the ways in which Google's DeepMind has partnered with the UK's National Health Service (NHS) are examples of how synergy between tech giants and healthcare providers can spark innovation.

The Human Element

No matter how advanced GAI becomes, human judgment, empathy, and expertise will remain paramount. GAI systems can process vast amounts of data, optimize treatment plans, and even foresee complications, but they cannot replace the nuanced understanding and compassion that skilled healthcare professionals bring to the table. The most promising future scenarios involve AI augmenting human roles rather than supplanting them.

Continuous Learning and Adaptation

As the role of AI and GAI expands, continuous learning will be essential—not only for the models themselves but also for the medical workforce. Clinicians and administrators must stay abreast of advancements in AI, while developers and data scientists should deepen their understanding of clinical workflows and patient needs. This cyclical relationship can foster AI systems that evolve in tandem with real-world healthcare practices, closing the gap between theoretical potential and practical implementation.

Final Thoughts

In this chapter, we have delved into the possible future directions and innovations that GAI could bring to healthcare. From predictive modeling and personalized medicine to AI-driven drug design, synthetic data generation, and beyond, the potential is vast. The marriage of GAI with wearable technology, the Internet of Things, and telehealth platforms promises continuous, patient-centric care. Meanwhile, the prospect of AI-augmented robotics, VNAs, and adaptive clinical trials portends an era of rapid, dynamic advancements in both diagnosis and treatment.

However, this future is not without its complexities. Ethical challenges, regulatory obstacles, and the importance of maintaining patient trust underscore the need for deliberate, collaborative approaches. Ensuring equitable access to these technologies, upholding the highest standards of data privacy, and preserving the critical human element in healthcare delivery must remain at the forefront of all advancements.

As we look toward the horizon, one thing is clear: GAI's role in healthcare will continue to expand and evolve, pushing the boundaries of what is possible in medicine. The groundbreaking innovations on the horizon have the potential to usher in a new era where healthcare is more accessible, precise, and patient-focused than ever before. For patients, this may translate into more personalized care, improved outcomes, and a stronger sense of agency over their own health.

For clinicians and healthcare systems, GAI can enhance efficiency, reduce burdens, and open up unprecedented avenues for research and collaboration.

In many ways, we are witnessing the dawn of a transformation that will shape the healthcare of tomorrow. As we progress through this book, we will continue to explore the nuances, benefits, and challenges of this rapidly changing landscape. The future, shaped by GAI, is poised to be one of ongoing discovery, collaboration, and, most importantly, improved care for patients across the globe.

Now that we have taken a detailed look at the future landscape of GAI in healthcare and where this all could be going, let's explore the top companies and key players who are driving the innovation that may take us there.

Chapter 4

Key Players and Startup Opportunities

> *There's a certain feeling that happens when a new technology adjusts your thinking about computing. Google did it. Firefox did it. AWS did it. iPhone did it. OpenAI is doing it with ChatGPT.*
>
> **Aaron Levie**

The healthcare industry's rapid pivot toward leveraging Gen AI is shaped not just by new breakthroughs in technology but also by the ecosystem of key players—big tech companies, academic powerhouses, nimble startups, and influential venture capitalists—who are collectively driving innovation. This chapter will delve into the major organizations, institutions, and emerging ventures leading the charge in generative AI (GAI) for healthcare. We will also explore the unique collaborative relationships forming between tech giants and academic research centers and how those relationships foster an environment ripe for startup development. Finally, we will look at the critical success factors for GAI startups, examine real-world examples, and offer guidance for aspiring entrepreneurs looking to join this dynamic space.

"The path to an optimal health delivery system made possible by AI progress is clear: embrace GAI as the foundation of future medical practice and turn the *practice* of medicine into the *science* of medicine," said Vinod Khosla. "With Gen AI, each cancer patient would get the benefit of the last thousand peer-reviewed publications on their cancer, filtered through AI and human judgment. Each cardiac patient's type and dose of blood thinner can be modulated by the deluge

 DOI: 10.4324/9781003665434-4

of their genomic or transcriptomic data appropriately applied and simplified by the AI, and titrated by the AI through ongoing patient conversations, appropriately adjusted for the patient's lifestyle and physician-approved care plan. With AI, all of medical literature and all of data-intensive medicine, which would overwhelm human physicians, would be available to apply to every patient care plan."

As you might imagine, all the big players in tech are now totally immersed in Gen AI. Google, Microsoft, IBM, Apple, and Oracle are all heavily invested in GAI and are actively involved in developing their own solutions or partnering with other companies or academia to unleash the next big thing. Besides being some of the best-known names in the tech industry, if you look for the binding thread that all of these companies have in common when it comes to GAI, you will find that they have all come to the realization that GAI has put the power of AI into a format where everyone can use it. You do not have to rely on coding to create or leverage an AI application. What that means is that these tech innovators can dream up what they will and not be held back by the notion of "How will we ever program that?" or "That's a great idea, but it will take a staff of dozens of engineers working around the clock to code even the front end of that kind app." Those days are gone, particularly when you bring in the power of the multi-agent systems we mentioned in our last chapter. If you speak to any of the CEOs from these companies, they will all say the same thing—the floodgates of innovation are open wide now that we do not have to rely on a team of PhD-level people to create new GAI tools.

The other thing that they all have in common is their recognition of the value of forming partnerships with other big players in tech, hardware, cloud infrastructure, and academia.

Major Companies Driving GAI in Healthcare

Google Health

Overview and History

Google's involvement in healthcare has expanded significantly over the past decade, culminating in the establishment of Google Health. While Google's primary roots lie in search and advertising, the company has long recognized the potential of advanced AI and machine learning to solve complex problems. The reorganization into Alphabet in 2015 gave Google more freedom to invest in "moonshots," many of which revolve around medical AI. DeepMind, which Google acquired in 2014, has contributed heavily to breakthroughs in generative models and reinforcement learning.

Projects and Impact

A notable accomplishment is Google's work on AI-assisted diagnostics, especially in medical imaging. For instance, Google researchers published studies on diabetic retinopathy detection using deep learning algorithms that match or exceed human specialists' performance. Although these were not purely "generative" in nature, they set the stage for broader AI-driven healthcare solutions. More recently, Google has showcased generative language models like LaMDA and the subsequent PaLM variations, some of which are being explored for summarizing medical literature, assisting with clinical note-taking, and even generating synthetic patient data for research.

In May of 2025, Google Health announced the launch of MedGemma, which the company says contains the most capable open models that help developers build healthcare-based AI applications to examine medical images, generate medical image reports, triage patients, and answer questions about medical images.

The company also announced at Google I/O 2025 that Google's Health Connect will soon be compatible with Runna, Mi Fitness, and Garmin.

Google Health Connect, which was launched back in 2022, is Android's Apple Health equivalent. It allows you to easily share health metrics and fitness data across devices and between apps, while privacy controls allow you to choose what data is and isn't shared. According to Google starting in June, Mi Fitness (Xiaomi's fitness wearable app), Runna (the excellent running coach app that Strava recently acquired), and Garmin will be able to share data with Health Connect, as revealed on its Android Stage, and spotted by Android Central.

Collaborations

Google Health is also known for forging partnerships with major healthcare providers and research institutions, such as the Mayo Clinic and the National Health Service (NHS) in the UK. These collaborations often involve exploring ways to embed AI-driven analysis within clinical workflows—something that, as we saw in previous chapters, is crucial for real-world adoption. The combination of Google's computational firepower and the domain expertise of clinical institutions holds immense promise for future GAI innovations, including predictive modeling, drug discovery, and large-scale public health initiatives.

IBM

IBM Watson's Healthcare Journey

IBM Watson made headlines nearly a decade ago by winning the quiz show "Jeopardy!"—a triumph of natural language processing (NLP) that many saw as the dawn of AI's mainstream acceptance. Soon after, IBM directed significant efforts toward applying Watson's capabilities to healthcare. Watson for Oncology, for instance, was designed to offer clinical decision support, suggesting personalized treatment plans for cancer patients.

Current Focus on Generative AI

While IBM has gradually scaled back some of Watson Health's more ambitious offerings, citing difficulties in data integration and the complexities of navigating healthcare markets, the company continues to research advanced AI models. IBM's interest in GAI has grown as large language models (LLMs) show promise in synthesizing vast amounts of medical data into coherent insights. The newly revitalized focus is on enterprise-grade AI platforms that can aid hospitals with administrative, clinical, and operational tasks.

Lessons Learned and Ongoing Strategy

One of the key lessons from IBM's earlier efforts in healthcare AI was the importance of reliable, high-quality data. This challenge remains central to any organization dabbling in GAI. IBM is also emphasizing explainable AI—a critical factor for clinical environments where black-box models may not be widely trusted. Their research now includes exploring how generative models can produce transparent, auditable outputs that clinicians can understand and verify, making adoption more likely and more ethically sound.

NVIDIA

NVIDIA is emerging as a major cornerstone in building the GAI-centric future of healthcare we espoused in the last chapter. NVIDIA may not be a traditional healthcare brand, but its role in shaping the GAI revolution is immense. Known for designing graphics processing units (GPUs) originally tailored for gaming, the company quickly adapted its hardware to perform high-performance computing tasks, including deep learning and generative modeling.

NVIDIA is an interesting case to look at because they were not traditionally known as software developers like the others on this list but a chipmaker. Yet they recognized early on the huge contribution they could make to GAI by becoming something more.

This is why, right now, they are so far out ahead of everybody. Apple, Oracle, Microsoft, and all the software companies knew they were going to need faster, more powerful chips to implement their GAI innovations. They would have to go to a company like NVIDIA for that. NVIDIA already had the chip technology, so they had the foresight to marry it to their own GAI applications. This way, they went from being known only as an IT infrastructure company to one that could create an all-encompassing "GAI ecosystem" built on their powerful chip technology. That is why they are the flagship driving GAI innovation and why their stocks have been soaring in recent years.

Today, NVIDIA's GPUs and software development kits (like CUDA and TensorRT) are foundational in training sophisticated neural networks at scale.

Clara Platform and GAI

NVIDIA has expanded directly into healthcare with its Clara platform, which offers an ecosystem of software tools and AI models that address medical imaging, genomics, and patient monitoring. Within the GAI realm, Clara Guardian and related toolkits are increasingly used to develop synthetic healthcare data, generate complex 3D medical images, and optimize various machine learning workflows. By accelerating the training and inference processes, NVIDIA's hardware and software solutions are powering much of the behind-the-scenes computational heavy lifting for advanced GAI initiatives.

Partnerships and Influence

NVIDIA's influence extends through partnerships with universities and healthcare startups. By offering early-stage companies grants, technical support, and access to cutting-edge hardware, NVIDIA fosters an ecosystem where GAI can thrive. Their presence at healthcare conferences and investment in specialized developer programs underscores NVIDIA's commitment to this domain and cements its status as a key enabler of GAI-driven healthcare solutions.

Oracle

Expansion into Healthcare

Oracle, traditionally known for its database software and enterprise solutions, has made significant inroads into healthcare through strategic acquisitions and product development. The acquisition of Cerner in 2022 marked a pivotal step, positioning Oracle as a formidable player in the electronic health records (EHR) domain—an area critical for AI implementation and data aggregation.

GAI's Role in Oracle's Vision

Oracle's robust data management tools and cloud infrastructure provide a natural foundation for developing and deploying advanced AI models, including GAI. Through Cerner's extensive footprint in hospitals and health systems, Oracle now has access to large-scale clinical data, enabling the company to explore predictive modeling, patient flow optimization, and synthetic data generation.

Integrations and Partnerships

Oracle focuses on integrating GAI solutions directly into EHR workflows, aiming to enhance data-driven decision-making for clinicians. By leveraging its vast enterprise ecosystem and cloud services, Oracle can help health systems implement AI-driven solutions without uprooting existing infrastructure. Partnerships with public agencies and academic institutions further bolster Oracle's ability to apply GAI for large-scale population health initiatives, such as chronic disease management or pandemic response planning.

Meta

AI Research Roots and Strategic Shift

Formerly Facebook, Meta commands one of the world's most robust AI research organizations through its Fundamental AI Research (FAIR) group. Although Meta's public image often centers on social networking, its deep-learning breakthroughs such as computer-vision architectures like ResNet to large-language models such as LLaMA, feed directly into healthcare-oriented initiatives. The company's open-science stance, which includes publishing model weights and code, has accelerated academic and startup experimentation in medical NLP and imaging.

Key Healthcare Projects

Meta's *AI for Open Science* team collaborates with New York University's Langone Health on fastMRI, a project that uses generative models to reconstruct higher-resolution MRI images from shorter scan times, potentially reducing patient discomfort and scanner bottlenecks. Meta Reality Labs researchers have also worked on EMG-based neural-interface wearables that decode motor-intent signals, technology that may one day power prosthetics or rehabilitation devices. In the clinical-language space, Meta's LLaMA and related models are already being fine-tuned by external partners for automated chart summarization and anonymized de-identification of physician notes.

Privacy and Federated-Learning Focus

Given Meta's scrutiny over data use, the company has taken a federated-learning approach in several healthcare pilots, keeping patient data inside hospital firewalls while sharing only encrypted model updates. By doubling down on differential-privacy research and secure multiparty computation, Meta positions itself as a supporter of privacy-preserving Gen AI pipelines—an asset for institutions wary of sending PHI to external clouds.

Apple

Consumer-Centric Approach to Healthcare

Apple's influence in healthcare has grown considerably through consumer devices such as the Apple Watch and the Health app. While Apple has not branded itself as a traditional healthcare company, its massive user base and emphasis on data privacy uniquely position it to impact AI-driven healthcare solutions.

Leveraging GAI and User Data

The Apple Watch's built-in sensors can capture health metrics like heart rate, ECG readings, blood oxygen levels, and activity tracking. By securely analyzing these data points with AI algorithms, Apple has the potential to generate personalized health insights for millions of users. Recent iOS updates have introduced features like fall detection and irregular heart rhythm notifications—capabilities that may one day evolve into more sophisticated generative models predicting future health events or designing personalized wellness plans.

Collaborations and Future Directions

Apple collaborates with research institutions via initiatives such as the Apple Heart and Movement Study, the Women's Health Study, and others. These collaborations gather longitudinal data from diverse populations, creating fertile ground for developing GAI models. Apple's unwavering stance on user privacy, highlighted by on-device data processing for sensitive information, could set a new standard for "privacy-preserving AI." In the coming years, Apple may well expand its focus to more deeply integrate GAI in health monitoring and early disease detection, potentially transforming the consumer-healthcare interface.

Amazon

Amazon Web Services (AWS) underpins thousands of hospital IT stacks, making Amazon a significant player in healthcare AI. The AWS HealthLake platform converts raw clinical data into machine-readable FHIR format, a prerequisite for training generative models that need clean, structured inputs. AWS also offers Bedrock and SageMaker services that let organizations fine-tune large-language models or diffusion-based image generators under HIPAA-eligible environments.

Alexa and Ambient Clinical Interfaces

Building on the reach of Alexa smart speakers, Amazon has piloted voice-first elder-care programs that remind users to take medication, log vitals, or connect with telehealth portals. In hospital settings, Alexa Smart Properties integrate with nurse call systems, letting patients request assistance or educational content hands-free. GAI upgrades now aim to turn these scripted interactions into more conversational, context-aware exchanges—effectively a virtual bedside agent.

Clinic and Pharmacy Expansion

Through acquisitions such as PillPack and the launch of Amazon Clinic, the company is venturing into direct patient services. GAI supports asynchronous chat consultations by summarizing patient-entered symptom narratives for telehealth clinicians, while back-office agents automate prior-authorization paperwork and prescription fulfillment. In logistics, Amazon's optimization engines—originally built for e-commerce—are being repurposed to route urgent meds and medical devices, illustrating how supply-chain Gen AI can cut delivery times for home-care patients.

Partnership Ecosystem

Similar to its cloud rivals, Amazon cultivates a marketplace of partner algorithms on AWS Marketplace. Healthcare ISVs can deploy pre-trained generative models—radiology report generators, pathology slide interpreters, synthetic-data engines—directly into an AWS tenant, inheriting Amazon's security and compliance certifications. This plug-and-play approach accelerates experimentation for health systems that lack in-house AI talent.

Microsoft

Cloud Infrastructure for Healthcare AI

Microsoft has been ramping up its footprint in healthcare, primarily through its Azure cloud platform. Azure offers specialized healthcare data management solutions that comply with regulations like HIPAA and GDPR. Coupled with services such as Azure Machine Learning, Microsoft is well-positioned to offer end-to-end infrastructure for GAI development, covering data ingestion, training, deployment, and monitoring.

Nuance Acquisition and Clinical Applications

A major leap for Microsoft came in 2021 with its acquisition of Nuance Communications, a leader in conversational AI and ambient clinical intelligence. Nuance's Dragon Medical is already widely used for clinical documentation, and the combined expertise is setting the stage for advanced generative language models that can streamline and possibly automate much of the administrative overhead in healthcare. This might include generating comprehensive patient notes from clinician-patient conversations or creating synthetic patient datasets for research while preserving privacy.

Microsoft Research Collaborations

Microsoft also invests heavily in academic partnerships to foster the next wave of AI talent and innovation. Initiatives like AI for Health provide grants and technical expertise to researchers tackling global health challenges, including those related to the COVID-19 pandemic. By nurturing these partnerships, Microsoft helps advance the entire GAI ecosystem and ensures that ethical and inclusive frameworks guide technology's development.

Research and Academic Leaders in AI Development

Massachusetts Institute of Technology (MIT)

Pioneering Research

MIT is synonymous with cutting-edge technology, and its involvement in AI spans decades. Labs like the MIT Computer Science and Artificial Intelligence Laboratory (CSAIL) and the Abdul Latif Jameel Clinic for Machine Learning in

Health (J-Clinic) are at the forefront of developing new AI architectures, including generative adversarial networks (GANs), variational autoencoders (VAEs), and transformer models. Much of their work has direct applicability to healthcare, such as using GAI to detect patterns in omics data or to create synthetic medical images.

Collaborations with Industry

MIT's strength also lies in forging partnerships with industry leaders, enabling the translation of theoretical work into practical solutions. Collaborations with companies like Pfizer, Novartis, and IBM have yielded research on drug discovery, personalized medicine, and advanced diagnostics. Through these alliances, students and faculty gain access to real-world problems and large datasets, fueling more robust experimentation in generative models.

Harvard University and Harvard Business School (HBS)

Interdisciplinary Approach

Harvard University, and particularly Harvard Medical School (HMS), has a storied history of medical breakthroughs. In recent years, Harvard faculty and affiliates have increasingly turned to AI to address clinical challenges. Initiatives like the HMS Center for Computational Biomedicine focus on large-scale data analysis, while other programs incorporate generative modeling to simulate complex disease mechanisms.

Harvard Business School (HBS) adds another layer to the conversation: While HMS and MIT might focus on the technical aspects of GAI, HBS frequently looks at the market, financial, and organizational challenges of implementing AI solutions. The synergy between these schools fosters an environment where tech, medicine, and business perspectives can converge.

Startup Incubators and Accelerators

Harvard also supports various incubator and accelerator programs aimed at commercializing research. The Harvard Innovation Labs (i-lab) provides resources for student and faculty-led startups, offering mentorship and funding opportunities. This ecosystem fosters the birth of new GAI-driven healthcare ventures, bridging academic research and real-world application.

Other Academic Heavyweights

In addition to MIT and Harvard, numerous other institutions drive the evolution of GAI in healthcare:

- **Stanford University**: Stanford's AI Lab and the Stanford Institute for Human-Centered AI (HAI) have produced seminal work in NLP, computer vision, and emerging fields like AI ethics. Their proximity to Silicon Valley creates a direct pipeline for commercializing cutting-edge research.
- **Johns Hopkins University**: Known for its medical school and research facilities, Johns Hopkins harnesses AI for patient care, epidemiology, and health policy. Their interdisciplinary approach often fuses clinical expertise with data science.
- **University of Toronto**: A cradle of deep learning innovations, U of T's Vector Institute has been influential in foundational AI research. Collaborations with hospitals like the University Health Network create robust opportunities for healthcare-focused GAI projects.

Key Partnerships Between Tech Leaders and Academia

As important as the partnerships, acquisitions, and support of startups are among and between tech companies, the importance of the contribution of academia cannot be understated.

MIT, the HBS, Caltech, Stanford, and others all serve as fountains of talent and cutting-edge research that could yield Gen AI tools that could be commercially licensed to the tech firms for them to further develop and bring to market. Say an academic think tank proposes a remarkable idea for a GAI application. The academic center will do the research and write the papers on it; they may even file for the patents on it, but then they need to work with either the startups or the big companies that have vast amounts of money to make it commercial.

Industry-Funded Research

Many of the most promising breakthroughs in GAI come from projects co-funded by industry and academic partners. For example, the MIT-IBM Watson AI Lab is a $240 million partnership dedicated to advancing AI hardware and software, with a significant emphasis on healthcare applications. Similarly, Microsoft's AI for Health program has funded research at various universities studying everything from global health challenges to hospital resource optimization.

Incubation Labs and Innovation Centers

A growing trend is the creation of joint innovation centers where academic researchers work side by side with industry engineers. Google's collaborations with institutions like the University of California, San Francisco (UCSF), or the Mayo Clinic exemplify this approach. By embedding Google employees in a clinical setting, these labs accelerate the time from proof of concept to pilot testing. Similarly, at Stanford's Byers Center for Biodesign, students and faculty collaborate with medical device companies to explore novel technologies, including GAI, for healthcare innovation.

Talent and Intellectual Property (IP) Considerations

Such partnerships often raise complex questions about ownership of intellectual property. While universities typically aim to publish results openly, corporate partners may seek to patent new algorithms or technologies. Balancing open science with commercial interests is an ongoing challenge—one that shapes how quickly GAI advances in healthcare and how accessible those innovations will be to the public.

Startup Opportunities in GAI for Healthcare

What does all this market takeover, cooperation, and collaboration by Big Tech mean for startups? Does it inhibit innovation or open the door for startups?

Perhaps surprisingly, it is a little of both. The big players have a lot of money and muscle behind them, which could seem intimidating to a startup, but they are also hungry for the next big thing. Like always, the best move for any startup is to get noticed by and eventually acquired by one of the big fish.

Let's look at ambient listening technology as an example. Long before any of you heard of ChatGPT, there was a company called Nuance that developed the best-known and most used "speech to text" medical dictation software known as Dragon. It was a game-changer when it came to digitizing doctor's notes, and it was soon integrated with EMRs and was a precursor to the kinds of things that are being done with ambient listening in clinical settings now.

In March of 2022, Microsoft acquired Nuance. It was an all-cash transaction worth $19.7 billion, making it the largest tech M&A deal in 2021 and the largest all-cash tech M&A deal since 2018.

Since the acquisition, Microsoft has rolled out Dragon Ambient eXperience, or DAX, its premier clinical ambient listening tool. Several large healthcare systems like the University of Michigan Health-West, WellSpan Health, and Providence Health Care are utilizing DAX. According to KLAS Research, it is very popular among doctors and has been ranked number one in KLAS Emerging Solutions Top 20 reports for improving clinician experiences.

The takeaway is this. Startups with impressive needs for GAI technologies like ambient listening will be well-funded. Well-funded startups will succeed and get picked up on the radar of Google, Microsoft, etc., and will thrive, while others may drop off or may need to seek the help of facilitators and incubators.

Current VC Investment Trends

Venture capital funding for AI-enabled healthcare has been on a steady upward trajectory, with billions of dollars invested annually. Within this broader category, GAI-focused startups are drawing particular attention, especially in areas like:

- **Drug Discovery and Precision Medicine**: Investors are attracted to the potential for short-circuiting traditional R&D timelines. AI-driven methods can theoretically identify viable candidates in a fraction of the time, reducing cost and risk.
- **Diagnostics and Medical Imaging**: While this field already has established players, there remains considerable room for growth, particularly in developing generative models that augment data or generate synthetic images for training.
- **Healthcare Administration**: Whether it's automating coding, billing, or medical documentation, GAI can significantly reduce administrative burdens. Startups offering solutions in this domain often appeal to providers looking to cut costs.

High-profile venture capital firms such as Andreessen Horowitz, Sequoia Capital, and General Catalyst regularly invest in healthcare AI. More specialized healthcare-focused funds, like Foresite Capital, define their portfolios by their emphasis on next-gen diagnostics, digital health platforms, and AI-driven drug discovery. With GAI at the frontier, many of these investors are seeking founders who can demonstrate both technical acumen and a nuanced understanding of clinical challenges.

Emerging White Spaces

While certain segments like medical imaging or drug discovery are already relatively crowded, several niches remain underexplored:

1. **Preventive Care and Wellness**: Developing generative models that predict individual health trajectories and generate personalized care plans could be a massive area of growth, particularly if integrated with wearable and IoT data.

2. **Mental Health and Behavioral Change**: AI chatbots for mental health already exist, but truly generative models that adapt personalized interventions, track subtle psychological cues, and engage users empathetically are still in the early phases.
3. **Public Health Management**: GAI systems capable of simulating pandemics, resource allocation, and population-level interventions could be invaluable for government agencies and NGOs. COVID-19 highlighted the urgent need for robust simulation and planning tools, and GAI could fill that gap.
4. **Medical Education and Training**: GAI-driven simulations and synthetic data sets can revolutionize how medical students and residents learn. Startups focused on creating advanced training modules and VR/AR simulations stand to make a significant impact.

Incubators, Accelerators, and Resources

Aspiring entrepreneurs can tap into various healthcare- and AI-focused accelerators; here are a few:

- **Y Combinator**: Although sector-agnostic, YC frequently invests in healthcare AI startups. Their three-month program provides seed funding, mentorship, and exposure to a vast network of investors.
- **Techstars Healthcare Accelerator**: Partnering with organizations like Cedars-Sinai or UnitedHealthcare, Techstars runs specialized programs focusing on digital health solutions, many of which involve advanced AI.
- **StartX Med (Stanford)**: A non-profit accelerator dedicated to Stanford-affiliated entrepreneurs, StartX Med has a strong track record of nurturing AI-driven healthcare ventures.
- **MassChallenge HealthTech**: Based in Boston, MassChallenge offers a vast network of mentors, corporate partners, and hospitals to help early-stage companies validate and scale.
- **GlobalVenturesX (GVX) Venture Studio:** GVX is an incubator focused on launching mission-driven startups that leverage technology to solve pressing challenges in healthcare. By nurturing ventures like FusionCare AI, GVX fosters innovation at the intersection of care and technology.
- **Accenture**: A global professional services firm, Accenture operates various innovation hubs and industry-focused programs that support AI adoption, including GAI solutions. Through Accenture Ventures, the company invests in and partners with promising startups, offering them strategic guidance, technical resources, and access to Accenture's extensive

client network across healthcare and life sciences. In particular, the firm's Applied Intelligence division provides expertise in data strategy, advanced analytics, and AI engineering, helping entrepreneurs integrate GAI solutions into complex enterprise environments. Accenture often collaborates with healthcare institutions to prototype and pilot emerging AI applications, bridging the gap between conceptual research and real-world implementation.

In addition to these accelerators, entrepreneurs can look to research consortia, online communities, and open-source AI frameworks (such as TensorFlow or PyTorch) to jumpstart product development. Public datasets from the NIH, NHS, and academic institutions offer invaluable training data, although as we've noted, privacy and regulatory compliance are paramount.

Of course, you can always work with a consulting firm like ours, BigRio. We pride ourselves on helping healthcare organizations, large and small, with Gen AI adoption and digital transformation. We have been working with companies across the healthcare industry to implement digital initiatives, from EHRs that streamline data management to telehealth platforms that bridge geographical gaps, enabling the innovative solutions that drive digital transformation strategy. Leading healthcare IT innovator Vivid Health recently partnered with BigRio to use our proprietary GAI solution, Odyssey Accelerator, to develop an LLM-driven end-to-end solution that can assess a patient's status on any combination of more than 100 chronic conditions across sixteen specialties, generating personalized care plans at scale in under 30 seconds. That's over 75 million possible care plan combinations in a fraction of the time it typically takes to pull together individualized plans.

Vivid Health's GAI-driven care management platform is currently the most powerful on the market. Its successful development and deployment stand as a testament to GAI's potential to enhance the quality and efficiency of healthcare delivery.

Navigating Challenges and Seizing Opportunities

Data Accessibility and Privacy

Startups aiming to build GAI models for healthcare will likely struggle with data access. Healthcare data is highly regulated, and institutions are often hesitant to share patient information without strict governance. Synthetic data can partially address these concerns, but ensuring that synthetic data still represents real-world diversity and complexity is no trivial task. Entrepreneurs must devise robust data-sharing agreements and de-identification processes and comply with frameworks like HIPAA, GDPR, or emerging laws that might govern AI in healthcare more directly.

Interoperability with Existing Systems

Hospital IT environments are famously fragmented, relying on legacy systems that do not always speak a common language. For GAI tools to integrate seamlessly, they must be designed with interoperability in mind. Standards like FHIR (Fast Healthcare Interoperability Resources) are making inroads, but real-world implementation remains patchy. Successful startups typically build robust APIs, tailor their software for EHR vendors like Epic or Cerner, and test extensively in live clinical settings.

Ensuring Clinical Validation and Trust

Clinical validation is more than a regulatory box to tick; it's a marker of credibility for both providers and patients. For GAI models, traditional validation methodologies, like prospective studies or randomized controlled trials, may need adaptation. For instance, a GAI-based system that creates synthetic patient data or "inventive" drug molecules may require entirely new evaluation criteria. Startups must work closely with academic medical centers or specialized research organizations that can rigorously test AI performance against established clinical metrics.

Funding and Exit Strategies

Securing funding is just the start. Many healthcare AI startups need multiple rounds of investment before they can market a fully compliant, validated product. Exit strategies can include acquisition by larger healthcare tech companies, integration into pharmaceutical giants, or an initial public offering (IPO). Given the growing interest in AI, big tech might aggressively seek to acquire smaller GAI ventures to fill strategic gaps in their offerings—a development that entrepreneurs should keep on their radar when charting a long-term vision.

Startup Success in the GAI Healthcare Arena

What Makes for a Successful GAI Startup?

At the heart of any successful GAI startup lies robust technical expertise. Founders need to be adept in AI frameworks, data engineering, and healthcare-specific regulations. A promising GAI healthcare startup must build solutions that can integrate with existing clinical workflows, handle sensitive patient data securely, and generate tangible insights or outcomes.

Domain Expertise and Clinical Partnerships

Healthcare is a complex industry with high stakes. Startups that lack medical domain expertise or fail to collaborate closely with clinicians often struggle to gain traction. The most successful ventures typically have strong advisory boards featuring physicians, regulatory experts, and healthcare administrators. These advisors guide the product roadmap, ensuring the startup's GAI solutions solve real clinical problems rather than hypothetical ones.

Clear Regulatory Strategy

Regulatory hurdles, particularly when dealing with clinical decision support or medical devices, can stall even the most promising technologies. Successful GAI startups plan for FDA or CE Mark approvals (in Europe) early in their development cycle. They engage with regulators, gather clinical evidence, and build solutions that comply with privacy laws like HIPAA and GDPR. A forward-thinking regulatory strategy can help startups avoid pitfalls and ensure smoother market entry.

Scalable Business Model

In healthcare, economic sustainability is paramount. GAI startups often rely on software-as-a-service (SaaS) models, subscription fees, or licensing deals. To succeed, they must show healthcare institutions that the adoption of their solution will lead to cost savings, efficiency gains, or improved patient outcomes. Demonstrating a measurable return on investment (ROI) is critical to convincing hospitals and insurers to invest in emerging technologies.

Real-World Examples of Successful GAI-Focused Startups

Insilico Medicine

Overview

Hong Kong-based **Insilico Medicine** focuses on GAI for drug discovery. By integrating biological data with advanced machine learning, Insilico aims to reduce the timelines and costs of finding viable drug candidates.

Core Technology

Insilico uses GANs and reinforcement learning to propose novel molecular structures likely to exhibit specific therapeutic properties. This approach has caught the attention of numerous pharmaceutical firms, which see it as a path to accelerate drug development cycles.

Hippocratic AI

Overview

Founded in February 2023, **Hippocratic AI** has quickly gained recognition for its bold and innovative approach to GAI in healthcare. The company's core mission is to leverage state-of-the-art LLMs and other generative techniques to simplify clinical workflows, enhance diagnostic accuracy, and empower patients with data-driven insights—all while maintaining rigorous standards of privacy and compliance.

Key Contributions and Solutions

Hippocratic AI's product suite includes an intelligent data platform that synthesizes patient information from diverse sources (EHR, wearables, lab data) into a cohesive profile. A specialized generative model then translates these complex data points into understandable, actionable recommendations for both patients and providers. Notably, the company's platform emphasizes HIPAA-compliant design from the ground up, employing sophisticated de-identification protocols to ensure patient privacy.

Collaborations and Vision

Despite its relative youth, Hippocratic AI has already formed promising partnerships with university hospitals and large private healthcare networks. The company's robust development roadmap includes expansions into personalized medicine and real-time clinical decision support tools. Hippocratic AI's rapid rise testifies to the enormous market appetite for GAI-driven solutions that elegantly address both technological and regulatory hurdles.

Aidoc

Overview

Israeli startup **Aidoc** utilizes advanced AI to analyze medical images, helping radiologists identify critical findings more efficiently. Although Aidoc's mainstay is not purely generative modeling, its continued evolution may involve synthetic data generation to train and refine its detection algorithms.

Clinical Integration

Aidoc has secured multiple regulatory approvals and is widely deployed in hospitals globally, illustrating how a specialized focus on emergency and radiology imaging can lead to swift market penetration and tangible clinical outcomes.

Owkin

Overview

French-American startup Owkin harnesses federated learning for collaborative medical research. Instead of centralizing sensitive patient data, Owkin allows hospitals to train AI models locally and share only the learned parameters.

Generative Dimension

While Owkin primarily emphasizes federated learning, the startup is researching generative models that create synthetic datasets for rare diseases, addressing the privacy concerns often associated with collaborative data science.

Atomwise

Overview

San Francisco-based Atomwise applies AI to structure-based drug design, examining protein-ligand interactions. By combining convolutional neural networks with medicinal chemistry, Atomwise accelerates early drug discovery and optimization.

Expanding Generative Horizons

Atomwise is exploring generative techniques to propose entirely new chemical structures. This forward-thinking strategy aligns with the broader healthcare trend of moving beyond pattern recognition to AI-driven innovation.

Advice for Aspiring GAI Healthcare Entrepreneurs

Validate the Clinical Need Early

Before writing a single line of code, entrepreneurs should confirm that there is a genuine clinical need for their solution. Interview clinicians, observe hospital workflows, and identify pain points that GAI can realistically address. Solutions that only marginally improve outcomes or that add complexity to already busy healthcare routines are less likely to gain traction.

Build a Balanced Team

A robust GAI healthcare startup requires a convergence of skill sets: AI and machine learning, clinical expertise, regulatory knowledge, and business acumen. Ideally, your founding team or key hires will cover all these bases. A lack in any one area can stall product development or prevent adoption in complex clinical ecosystems.

Embrace Iterative Prototyping and Pilot Projects

Healthcare institutions are often risk-averse, so demonstrating incremental success through pilot programs is key. Start small, prove efficacy in one department or with one patient population, and then scale. Use feedback from pilot sites to refine your generative models and user interfaces. This iterative approach builds trust and fosters strong institutional champions who can advocate for broader adoption.

Network Actively in the Healthcare Ecosystem

Conference attendance, especially at events like the Healthcare Information and Management Systems Society (HIMSS) conference or the Radiological Society of North America (RSNA) meeting, is critical to building relationships with healthcare leaders, clinicians, and potential partners. Industry groups, hackathons, and specialized AI and HealthTech meetups can also be valuable forums for connecting with investors, mentors, and early adopters.

Prioritize Ethics and Compliance

GAI can raise unique ethical questions. For instance, how does one ensure that synthetic data does not inadvertently re-identify real patients or that AI-generated treatment suggestions are equitable across diverse populations? Address these concerns head-on by setting up a dedicated ethics review panel or consulting with bioethicists. Proactive engagement with regulators and standard-setting organizations can also reduce future friction.

Final Thoughts

The world of GAI for healthcare is fueled by a vibrant ecosystem of key players—from global tech companies like Google, IBM, NVIDIA, and Microsoft to academic leaders such as MIT and Harvard University, to a burgeoning landscape of startups that are pushing boundaries in diagnostics, drug discovery, and beyond. These entities do not operate in isolation; their cross-pollinating partnerships, collaborations, and mutual support networks propel innovation forward at a remarkable pace.

The success of GAI-driven healthcare solutions hinges on more than just technical prowess. A deep understanding of clinical workflows, regulatory complexities, and healthcare economics is essential. Companies that excel in these areas—often guided by a board of clinicians, seasoned entrepreneurs, and AI experts—are those most likely to carve out meaningful roles in the healthcare sector. Venture capitalists and accelerators are also deeply invested in the potential of GAI, funneling resources into high-promise ventures and building specialized programs to mentor emerging founders.

For budding entrepreneurs, the path to launching a GAI-focused healthcare startup may be challenging, but it is also richly rewarding. The barriers to entry—data privacy concerns, complicated EHR integrations, and clinical validation—help ensure that only the most determined and well-prepared teams survive. Yet the payoff can be substantial: Beyond the commercial upside, successful startups have the potential to substantially improve healthcare delivery, reducing costs, enhancing patient outcomes, and even accelerating the pace of medical research.

As we progress through this book, remember that the interplay between established tech giants, academic powerhouses, and nimble startups is continuously reshaping the future of healthcare. Far from a zero-sum game, collaboration and co-innovation appear to be the guiding principles, offering countless opportunities for those willing to navigate the industry's complexities. The seeds planted by key players today will likely bear fruit in the form of GAI tools that redefine clinical practice, patient engagement, and overall health system efficiency. Whether you aspire to join a multinational enterprise, partner with a university research lab, or found your own GAI healthcare startup, an understanding of this ecosystem—and the factors that drive it—will be indispensable in forging a successful path forward.

In each of the last few chapters, concerns over ethics and privacy have underscored our discussions of innovation in GAI for healthcare. In our next chapter, we will take a much deeper look at this issue, and, to quote a famous arachnid superhero, see that "with great power comes great responsibility."

Chapter 5

Privacy and Ethical Considerations

Generative AI has unlocked exciting new avenues for artistic expression, content creation, and immersive storytelling. As this technology continues to evolve, it is essential to leverage its power responsibly and ensure its positive impact on society.

Mohith Agadi

In the preceding chapters, we have explored the transformative potential of generative AI (GAI) within healthcare. From predictive modeling and drug discovery to synthetic data generation and emerging startups, the possibilities appear limitless. However, with these vast opportunities come immense responsibilities, particularly concerning patient privacy, data security, and the ethical deployment of AI tools. In this chapter, we will delve into the complex landscape of privacy and ethics as it relates to GAI in healthcare. We will examine the challenges of maintaining patient confidentiality, discuss strategies for secure data sharing and anonymization, explore potential ethical dilemmas (including bias and fairness), and consider the intricacies of informed consent when AI is part of the diagnostic or treatment process. As GAI continues to reshape healthcare, understanding these ethical and privacy considerations is essential for long-term success and public trust.

Looking at the landscape of responsible AI (RAI) as it relates to Gen AI and healthcare, there are currently five major areas of concern:

1. Data privacy and patient confidentiality.
2. Ethical concerns.

DOI: 10.4324/9781003665434-5

3. Bias.
4. Governance and regulatory issues.
5. Trust in Gen AI by healthcare consumers.

During our interview, Dr. Priti Patel, Chief Medical Information Officer, John Muir Health System, shared that these indeed were reflective her own concerns.

> GenAI models risk amplifying biases already present in healthcare data. If training datasets are not representative, there's a danger of misdiagnoses or unfair treatment, particularly for underrepresented populations. This raises the critical question: Can we truly develop a model free of bias when the training data itself is flawed?

"Furthermore," she added, "the integration of GenAI tools in healthcare involves managing vast amounts of sensitive data, including Protected Health Information, Personally Identifiable Information, and intellectual property. As staff and providers increasingly use public or non-approved AI applications, the risk of data leakage grows. Even with rigorous compliance training, rapid adoption can outpace security measures, increasing vulnerability to data breaches and loss."

Let's take a look at each of these concerns.

Data Privacy and Patient Confidentiality

The Foundations of Patient Confidentiality

For centuries, healthcare providers have adhered to a code of confidentiality designed to protect patient information. This principle, historically grounded in the Hippocratic Oath, has been reinforced by modern regulations such as the Health Insurance Portability and Accountability Act (HIPAA) in the US and the General Data Protection Regulation (GDPR) in the European Union. These frameworks establish rules about data handling, access, storage, and dissemination, ensuring that individual medical information remains private and is disclosed only under specific, permissible circumstances.

With the rise of digital health records, telemedicine, and, more recently, GAI tools, the scope of patient privacy concerns has grown exponentially. Data is now generated and transferred at unprecedented speeds and volumes, prompting urgent questions about how best to preserve confidentiality in this new era.

The Challenge of GAI's Data Appetite

GAI models thrive on large, diverse datasets. The particular problem with Gen AI and LLMs is that their appetite for data is voracious and not very discriminatory, especially when we talk about publicly available tools like ChatGPT. These LLMs are designed to scan the internet and seek out and absorb whatever data they find relevant to a particular task. If private information happens to have been mistakenly loaded into a given database, and it gets scooped up in the process, so be it.

This becomes a major concern when leveraging LLMs for healthcare. To train a robust AI system capable of accurate or insightful results, whether for disease diagnosis, personalized medicine, or synthetic data generation, enormous amounts of patient data are often required. Examples of data inputs might include:

- Electronic Health Records (EHRs)
- Medical images (X-rays, MRIs, CT scans)
- Omics data (genomics, proteomics, metabolomics)
- Wearable and IoT device readings (heart rate, blood pressure, glucose levels)
- Clinical trial data (patient demographics, drug response rates)

The more comprehensive and varied the training data, the more powerful a GAI model can become. Yet this same data can be deeply personal and sensitive, raising serious privacy concerns if it is not managed correctly. A high-profile data breach or misuse of patient records can erode public trust in GAI, slow adoption, and even lead to legal repercussions.

Evolving Threats in a Digital Ecosystem

As data circulates among hospitals, research institutions, pharmaceutical companies, startups, and cloud service providers, new vulnerabilities emerge. Potential threats include:

- **Unauthorized Access or Hacking**: Cybercriminals may view aggregated healthcare data as extremely valuable, given the potential for identity theft or black-market trading of medical information.
- **Insider Threats**: Individuals within healthcare organizations could misuse privileged access to data.
- **Misconfigured Systems**: Even well-intentioned organizations can inadvertently expose data through improper configurations of cloud storage or APIs.

- **Re-identification Attacks**: Sophisticated algorithms can sometimes "re-identify" individuals from anonymized datasets by cross-referencing them with public records or other data sources.

When GAI models generate synthetic patient information, there is also a possibility—if not carefully controlled—of inadvertently encoding identifiable details within the synthetic output. If such synthetic data is publicly released, it could become a backdoor to real patient information.

Secure Data Sharing and Anonymization

Data sharing is a crucial enabler of advanced healthcare research. Multi-institution collaborations can rapidly accelerate AI development by pooling diverse patient populations, disease phenotypes, and care scenarios. For instance, global clinical databases can help AI researchers uncover rare disease patterns that might be invisible within a single hospital network. Additionally, startups like *Hippocratic AI* and other emerging companies often rely on partnerships with large health systems to refine and validate their GAI algorithms using more representative datasets.

Strategies for Secure Data Exchange

Organizations seeking to collaborate on GAI projects must prioritize security at every step. Key strategies include:

1. **Encrypted Communications**
2. End-to-end encryption (E2EE) ensures that data is protected during transit between parties. Encryption keys should be tightly controlled, and VPNs or dedicated secure channels can further reduce the risk of interception.
3. **Access Control and Role-Based Permissions**
4. Not every staff member or collaborator needs full access to the raw patient data. Implementing role-based access control (RBAC) ensures that each individual can only retrieve the data they specifically require for their role.
5. **Federated Learning**
6. Instead of pooling all data into a central repository, federated learning allows models to be trained locally at each data source. The aggregated model's parameters are shared and updated without transferring the underlying patient data. This technique enhances privacy while still benefiting

from multi-institutional datasets. The startup *Owkin*, profiled in a previous chapter, is a pioneer in federated learning for medical research.

7. **Edge Computing**
8. Similar to federated learning, edge computing processes data at or near its point of collection (e.g., wearable devices) rather than sending it to a central server. GAI tasks can be distributed across multiple local nodes to minimize large-scale data transfers.

De-Identification and Anonymization Techniques

Traditional anonymization involves removing direct identifiers (names, addresses, social security numbers). However, in an age of big data, "quasi-identifiers" like birth dates, zip codes, or unique clinical characteristics can still be traced back to individuals if combined with external databases. To address these concerns:

- **k-Anonymity**: Ensures that each record in a dataset is indistinguishable from at least k-1 other records regarding identifiable attributes.
- **L-Diversity**: Extends k-anonymity by ensuring that sensitive attributes within any anonymized group have a diversity of values, minimizing the risk of inferring sensitive details.
- **Differential Privacy**: Introduces statistical noise into the dataset or computations, making it mathematically improbable to reverse-engineer individual data from aggregate statistics.

GAI models themselves can also assist by producing **synthetic datasets** that mirror the statistical properties of real data without exposing actual patient records. Nonetheless, thorough validation is required to confirm that synthetic data does not inadvertently contain unique identifiers or patterns that could allow re-identification.

Medical Ethics and Using GAI for Healthcare Purposes

Balancing Innovation with Responsibility

The swift rise of GAI offers numerous benefits—improved diagnostic accuracy, personalized treatment, and operational efficiencies—but it also introduces ethical dilemmas that can be challenging to navigate. Unlike traditional rule-based systems, which follow explicitly programmed logic, generative models often learn from data in ways that humans struggle to fully interpret.

This "black box" quality can lead to concerns about accountability and the potential for unintended consequences.

Accountability and Liability

Who is responsible when something goes wrong? If a GAI tool recommends a treatment that leads to adverse patient outcomes, accountability might be shared among:

- The healthcare provider who used the tool,
- The AI developer or startup that created the model,
- The hospital or health system that integrated it into clinical workflows, or
- Potentially, even the data sources used to train the model, if they introduced biases or errors.

Regulatory bodies, such as the FDA in the US, have taken steps toward clarifying the classification of AI-based medical devices, but significant ambiguity remains. In some jurisdictions, the concept of "human oversight" is increasingly emphasized—requiring that a qualified professional remains in the loop for critical decisions, thereby maintaining accountability.

Informed Consent in AI-Driven Diagnosis and Treatment

Informed consent is a bedrock principle of medical ethics, requiring that patients understand the nature, benefits, and risks of a proposed treatment or procedure before agreeing to it. However, the integration of AI—and particularly GAI—into clinical decision-making complicates this process. Traditionally, consent conversations revolve around physician-led diagnoses and evidence-based treatment options. With AI in the mix, patients must also comprehend how the algorithm reached its recommendation and what limitations or uncertainties might accompany an AI-driven conclusion.

Transparency in AI Usage

Whether the AI tool is diagnosing skin lesions, suggesting personalized drug regimens, or generating synthetic data for research, *transparency* is essential for meaningful consent. Patients should be told:

- *AI is being used* in the diagnostic or decision-making process.
- *The role of the AI tool*—is it advisory, or is the clinician heavily reliant on it?

- *Are there any known limitations or biases* in the AI's model or dataset.
- *Potential risks* of AI-based recommendations, especially if they deviate from standard-of-care guidelines.

Practical Steps for Clinicians and Institutions

1. **Layperson-Friendly Explanations**
2. AI concepts—like deep learning or generative modeling—are notoriously complex. Clinicians can use analogies or simplified language to convey the AI's role in their practice. For example, describing GAI as a "smart assistant that looks at thousands of similar cases to find patterns" might foster better patient understanding than delving into neural network architectures.
3. **Decision Aids and Visualizations**
4. Interactive tools that show how an AI arrived at its recommendation can be invaluable. Simple visual outputs—like heatmaps that highlight significant regions in a medical image—can help patients see how the AI "views" their case. Some platforms also provide short text explanations.
5. **Shared Decision-Making**
6. In a patient-centered care model, AI's results should be framed as part of a collaborative dialogue. Patients, AI, and clinicians each bring unique insights. The final decision should reflect a synthesis of these inputs, respecting patient autonomy and clinical expertise.
7. **Documentation of AI Involvement**
8. Healthcare providers should document that AI was used during diagnosis or treatment planning. This record may have legal significance if disputes over accountability arise. It also helps maintain a transparent clinical workflow and fosters a culture of ethical responsibility.

The Black Box Problem

Deep learning models, particularly large neural networks used in GAI, often lack easy-to-understand explanations for their outputs. For example, if a generative model synthesizes a treatment plan for a rare cancer, the clinician may not know exactly which statistical correlations or data patterns led to that suggestion. In high-stakes healthcare settings, "explainability" is not just a buzzword—it's essential. Over-reliance on inscrutable AI systems can compromise informed decision-making, damage trust, and expose providers to legal and ethical risks. Efforts to build *explainable AI (XAI)* often involve developing methods that generate human-readable justifications or highlight the most influential variables shaping an AI's decisions.

Multi-Agent Systems and Ethical Complexity

As discussed in Chapter 4, multi-agent systems (MAS) distribute computational tasks among specialized agents—some generating patient data, others evaluating outcomes, and still others enforcing compliance. This approach can bolster robustness and reduce single points of failure. However, MAS architectures can also multiply ethical complexity. A breakdown in communication between agents or unethical emergent behaviors could introduce unforeseen outcomes. Clear protocols must define each agent's responsibilities, how they interact, and how accountability is assigned if an agent malfunctions or makes an inappropriate recommendation.

Bias and Fairness in AI Algorithms

The Roots of Bias

Bias in AI does not necessarily stem from malicious intent; more often, it arises from *imbalances or limitations in training data*. For instance, if an AI model designed to detect skin cancer is mostly trained on images of fair-skinned individuals, its accuracy may plummet when diagnosing darker-skinned patients. Such biases can lead to significant disparities in healthcare outcomes and can perpetuate systemic inequalities.

In a GAI context, bias can be amplified. LLMs, by their very nature, are more prone to bias because they almost "look for it" since they are very good at pattern matching. While bias has always been an issue for traditional AI, it is even a greater concern in Gen AI because it is much easier for bias to creep into an LLM-driven tool.

If a generative model is trained on skewed data, for example, limited demographic or geographic diversity, it may produce outputs that reinforce existing stereotypes or neglect the needs of underrepresented groups. For example, the CEO of Chanel, a British-Indian woman, Leena Nair, recently shared an experience on Instagram she had when she was invited to a demonstration of ChatGPT at Microsoft. She asked, "Show me the management team in a top luxury company." The image that ChatGPT generated was all men, including the CEO position. She said that, as a luxury brand with a woman CEO, she was stunned by this response. She said

> 70% of her clients are women; they have a woman CEO and many female board members, and yet ChatGPT is showing her an all-male executive team because it is picking up the intrinsic bias that 90% of all boardrooms, luxury brands or not, are male.

As you can see, the powerful predictive capabilities of GAI also amplify the ethical urgency to address data imbalances.

Consequences of Biased GAI

Biased generative models can have real-world implications:

1. **Inequitable Treatment Plans**: A GAI tool might repeatedly recommend more aggressive treatments for certain demographics due to historical bias in the dataset.
2. **Diagnostic Disparities**: Algorithms could fail to detect specific diseases in populations not well-represented in the training data, leading to delayed diagnoses.
3. **Misallocation of Resources**: Public health agencies using GAI for resource planning might inadvertently under-serve communities that are underrepresented in the data.

Such issues erode trust in AI-powered healthcare systems and can result in legal or reputational damage for the institutions that deploy them. For example, in 2019, a healthcare algorithm used in the U.S. was found to systematically underestimate the health needs of Black patients, spotlighting the need for thorough bias auditing.

Methods to Mitigate Bias

1. **Comprehensive and Diverse Datasets**
2. Strive to include representative data from different ethnicities, age groups, and socio-economic backgrounds. Healthcare organizations can form consortia to share diverse datasets, ensuring GAI models learn from a broad range of patient cases.
3. **Algorithmic Auditing**
4. Conduct bias audits that test AI outputs across demographic subgroups. Developers can apply statistical tools to measure disparities in prediction accuracy or recommended treatments. These audits should occur both pre-deployment and periodically post-deployment.
5. **Continuous Monitoring and Feedback Loops**
6. Healthcare data evolves over time, and so does bias. Implementing real-time performance monitoring helps identify shifts in model accuracy among specific populations. Corrective measures can then be applied, including retraining or refining the GAI models with updated datasets.

7. **Ethical Design Principles**
8. Some institutions adopt formal frameworks—like "Fairness, Accountability, and Transparency" (FAT) principles—to guide the development and deployment of AI systems. Having a structured set of guidelines can embed fairness considerations throughout the model lifecycle.
9. **Interdisciplinary Collaboration**
10. Bias mitigation often requires input from data scientists, ethicists, clinicians, and community representatives. Such collaboration ensures that technical solutions align with patient-centric goals and societal values.

Broader Ethical and Governance Structures

Role of Regulatory Bodies

Healthcare regulators worldwide are gradually issuing guidelines specific to AI and machine learning. The U.S. Food and Drug Administration (FDA) has introduced an "Artificial Intelligence/Machine Learning-Based Software as a Medical Device (SaMD) Action Plan," while the European Commission has proposed an Artificial Intelligence Act to classify AI tools by risk and define compliance requirements. These regulations aim to:

- Ensure the safety and effectiveness of AI tools.
- Promote transparency and accountability.
- Encourage ongoing performance monitoring and real-world evidence collection.

GAI, with its capacity to generate novel data or recommendations, falls into a more complex risk category. Regulatory bodies may require additional scrutiny around how GAI models are trained, validated, and updated over time.

Institutional Review Boards (IRBs)

IRBs (or Ethics Committees) are crucial in overseeing human-subject research, ensuring that studies meet ethical and regulatory standards. For AI-focused healthcare research, especially when using sensitive patient data, IRBs often require:

- Comprehensive risk assessments related to privacy, re-identification, and data security.
- Clarity on how synthetic or real patient data will be used, shared, or published.

- Explicit protocols for how patients are informed about AI involvement, particularly if used in experimental or investigational contexts.

As GAI projects become more prevalent, IRBs are updating their guidelines to address emerging scenarios, such as collaborative multi-site projects that involve data streaming, real-time model updates, and MAS coordinating tasks.

Professional Societies and Ethical Frameworks

Professional medical societies can offer domain-specific guidelines to ensure the ethical use of AI. For instance:

- *The American Medical Association (AMA)* has released guiding principles for AI integration in clinical settings.
- *The World Medical Association* is considering how the Declaration of Helsinki's ethical tenets apply to AI-mediated research.

Collaborative discussions across such organizations can help shape uniform standards, preventing fragmentation of ethical policies across different regions and specialties.

Case Study: Ethical Challenges in Real-World GAI Deployments

Hippocratic AI's Privacy-Centric Approach

As previously highlighted, Hippocratic AI exemplifies a startup committed to high standards of data privacy. Founded in early 2023, the company rapidly gained traction by offering HIPAA-compliant generative models that streamline clinical documentation, patient engagement, and data synthesis. One of Hippocratic AI's hallmark initiatives is its robust internal "Ethics and Compliance Committee," which reviews every new feature or dataset integration. By instituting privacy-by-design principles and conducting frequent bias audits, Hippocratic AI has built trust with hospital systems and payers, accelerating adoption.

Still, challenges persist. For instance, Hippocratic AI occasionally collaborates with academic partners for clinical trials involving rare diseases. These partnerships underscore the delicate balance between data sharing for medical breakthroughs and safeguarding patient confidentiality. Through federated learning and differential privacy techniques, Hippocratic AI mitigates re-identification risks while still benefiting from valuable data.

Multi-Agent Systems in Emergency Departments

An academic medical center in the US recently tested a *multi-agent GAI system* in its emergency department. One agent triaged patients based on EHR data, vital signs, and presenting symptoms; another generated diagnostic hypotheses; yet another compared these hypotheses against standard protocols; and a final agent offered logistical suggestions for bed management and resource allocation.

The pilot yielded efficiency gains and modest improvements in triage accuracy. However, ethical questions arose about patients who do not speak English or have atypical presentations. Some staff worried that the system's recommendations might inadvertently deprioritize non-English-speaking patients if the training data underrepresented that demographic. After discovering disparities in triage wait times, the system was taken offline for retraining with a more representative dataset, illustrating the crucial need for ongoing bias detection and correction.

The Path Forward: Building Trustworthy GAI Systems

Cultivating a Culture of Ethical Vigilance

In many healthcare organizations, ethical oversight is seen as an administrative hurdle. In the realm of GAI, however, ethical vigilance must be a *core value* woven into every stage of development and deployment. This can be fostered by:

- **Ethics Committees**: Regular meetings with cross-functional teams (clinicians, data scientists, legal experts, ethicists) to preemptively identify ethical red flags.
- **Transparent Reporting**: Publicly sharing information about data sources, model performance metrics, and any identified biases encourages community trust and provides opportunities for peer review.
- **Patient Advocacy**: Involving patient representatives in the design and testing phases of GAI tools ensures that real-world concerns and preferences shape the final product.

Proactive Compliance with Regulations

Given the fluid regulatory landscape, GAI developers must continuously track updates to laws and guidance. A proactive approach to compliance can be a competitive advantage, demonstrating due diligence to prospective clients and partners. Rather than viewing regulation as stifling, many forward-thinking developers collaborate with regulators early in the design process—seeking feedback, aligning on risk mitigation strategies, and even co-publishing best practices.

Ongoing Training and Education

Education is key to bridging the knowledge gap for both healthcare professionals and patients:

- **Clinician Training**: Physicians, nurses, and allied health professionals should receive regular updates on the capabilities, limitations, and ethical considerations of GAI tools. This can bolster confidence in AI-driven recommendations and enhance patient education.
- **Data Science Training**: AI developers coming from a purely technical background may lack awareness of healthcare's regulatory and ethical complexities. Interdisciplinary education that covers HIPAA, clinical workflows, and medical ethics can refine how GAI solutions are conceived and implemented.
- **Patient Outreach**: Healthcare systems can offer informational sessions, online resources, and demonstration tools that explain how GAI is being used. Engaged and informed patients are more likely to trust AI-assisted care.

Continuous Model Monitoring and Auditing

In the world of GAI, one-time validation is insufficient. Models must be continuously audited to detect performance drift, emerging biases, or new security vulnerabilities. This often requires:

- **Real-Time Analytics Dashboards**: Automated systems that track metrics like accuracy, false-positive rates, and demographic parity.
- **Scheduled Audits**: Periodic reviews of the model's outputs by multidisciplinary committees.
- **Feedback Loops**: Mechanisms that allow clinicians to flag suspicious AI suggestions or anomalies, ensuring that model retraining can incorporate this feedback.

A Matter of Trust

Even the most sophisticated privacy, security, and governance frameworks amount to little if patients and the broader public do not trust the technologies at hand. Against the backdrop of privacy breaches, algorithmic bias, and concerns about opaque "black-box" models, fostering trust in GAI has become a core challenge for both the tech and healthcare industries. As GAI tools gain traction in clinical decision-making, patient education, and health management, the onus is on solution providers and healthcare institutions to prove that these tools are not only effective but also safe, transparent, and respectful of human values.

Winning Hearts and Minds

A critical first step in earning public trust in GAI is clear and open communication with patients, as well as the clinicians who rely on AI-driven insights. When healthcare organizations integrate AI tools into their clinical workflows, they should avoid technical jargon and instead provide straightforward explanations of what these systems do, the scope of the data they process, and any relevant limitations or known biases. By offering easily understood narratives and examples, healthcare providers can bridge the gap between cutting-edge technology and everyday patient concerns, laying the foundation for trust.

Beyond fostering basic understanding, it is equally important to highlight evidence of the clinical value that AI can bring to healthcare settings. This means showcasing tangible outcomes, such as quicker diagnoses, reduced error rates, or enhanced personalization of care. Results from peer-reviewed research, randomized controlled trials, or large-scale pilot programs give patients and practitioners a basis for confidently embracing a new technology that has been proven to make a meaningful difference. Observing clear-cut benefits helps convert skepticism into a more open-minded stance on using AI, easing worries that machines might "overshadow" the human judgment critical to healthcare.

Professional validation further cements this trust. When influential organizations or leading academic institutions endorse AI tools, patients and practitioners become more willing to view them as reliable medical aids. The backing of professional societies or regulatory bodies, for instance, frames AI as a mainstream medical tool rather than an experimental or fringe innovation. The result is a broader acceptance, driven by the knowledge that respected authorities have thoroughly assessed the solution's accuracy and safety.

Guardrails and Safeguards

Equally vital to public confidence in GAI are the practical guardrails and safeguards that ensure AI functions responsibly. Key among these is the principle of human oversight—the notion that while AI might efficiently analyze vast amounts of data or generate detailed recommendations, a qualified healthcare professional retains ultimate authority over clinical decisions. Patients often find reassurance in knowing that their physicians are still at the helm, validating and contextualizing AI's outputs based on the patient's unique circumstances. By keeping humans "in the loop," healthcare systems preserve the foundational trust patients place in human expertise and empathy.

Regulatory reviews and certifications also serve as meaningful markers of reliability. When an AI tool successfully meets rigorous testing and accreditation requirements—comparable to those mandated for medical devices—it attains an elevated level of legitimacy. This structured approach ensures that AI is not merely a flashy novelty but a solution that has undergone careful scrutiny by regulators who share the public's interest in safety and efficacy. Furthermore, ethics committees and compliance teams within healthcare institutions provide a parallel layer of oversight by regularly auditing AI performance and requiring that developers maintain transparency about data usage, model biases, and documented outcomes.

Of equal importance is clarity about how patient data is collected, stored, and used. Transparent data practices build the foundation for informed consent and mitigate suspicions that patients' personal information might be exploited or mishandled. When data governance rules are explicitly stated, along with details about the scope of AI-driven analyses, patients are more apt to respect and accept the role of AI tools in their care. Taken together, these guardrails and safeguards help create a robust environment in which GAI can thrive without undermining the fundamental trust crucial to the patient-provider relationship.

Allies, Not Replacements: The Enduring Role of Human Expertise

When discussing AI in a broader societal context, a common fear is that technology will eventually supplant human roles, particularly in high-stakes fields like healthcare. The reality, however, is that GAI is fundamentally a tool meant to *augment* human expertise, not eliminate it. Just as telemedicine did not remove the need for doctors, generative models will not replace the nuanced judgments, empathy, and ethical considerations that clinicians bring to patient care.

Whether it's advising on a complex diagnosis or generating a personalized treatment plan, AI excels at quickly analyzing vast amounts of data and synthesizing patterns that might evade human cognition. However, healthcare ultimately depends on the interpersonal connection between provider and patient, including subjective assessments of a patient's condition, cultural and personal values, and the compassionate care that fosters healing beyond mere data points. Indeed, the ultimate safeguard that patients can rely on is precisely this human capacity for discernment. As GAI applications evolve and become more ubiquitous, the healthcare industry will continue to rely on the "human in the loop" principle as the ultimate line of defense and oversight.

In this light, far from heralding a dystopian future, GAI represents another step toward smarter, more efficient patient care—one in which clinicians have advanced tools at their disposal to improve outcomes, expedite treatments, and tailor care plans. Unlike the plot of various Sci-Fi movies and novels, "machines will not take over;" instead, they will serve as invaluable collaborators, freeing healthcare professionals to focus on the uniquely human aspects of medicine.

Final Thoughts

Privacy and ethics form the bedrock upon which GAI in healthcare must stand. Without robust safeguards, advanced AI tools risk betraying patient trust and fueling public skepticism, potentially undermining the remarkable progress documented in previous chapters of this book. Challenges abound, from the voracious data appetite of GAI models to the delicate balance between innovation and regulatory compliance. Yet the healthcare landscape also offers clear strategies and frameworks to address these concerns:

- *Securing data* through encryption, federated learning, and state-of-the-art anonymization.
- *Ensuring ethical deployment* by embracing transparency, informed consent, and ongoing bias audits.
- *Building fair models* that account for diverse patient populations, thereby avoiding the perpetuation of existing inequities.
- *Sustaining trust* through a culture of continuous auditing, interdisciplinary collaboration, and patient engagement.

In an era when MAS promise to magnify the potential of generative tools, diligent oversight is more crucial than ever. Each new agent or module introduced into the healthcare chain must adhere to stringent security and ethical standards, ensuring that the final product is not only innovative but also deeply respectful of patient well-being and autonomy.

As we look forward to the subsequent chapters in this book, it is worth remembering that the success of GAI in healthcare hinges not just on technical brilliance or financial investment but on the collective commitment of developers, clinicians, regulatory bodies, and patients to uphold privacy, fairness, and humanity. By addressing these ethical and privacy concerns head-on, we can unlock a future where GAI empowers better patient outcomes, reduces healthcare disparities, and enriches our understanding of medicine, without compromising the sacred trust that is at the heart of every healthcare interaction.

Chapter 6

Challenges in GAI Implementation

We need to design and build AI that helps healthcare professionals be better at what they do. The aim should be enabling humans to become better learners and decision-makers.

Mihaela van der Schaar, PhD

As we have seen thus far, Gen AI has captured the imagination of healthcare professionals, technology enthusiasts, policymakers, and patients around the world. The possibilities seem limitless: from generating synthetic patient data to improve models to assisting with drug discovery to supporting personalized patient care. Yet, for all its potential, generative AI (GAI) faces significant challenges when introduced into the complex, high-stakes environment of healthcare.

These challenges can be broadly categorized into technical hurdles, data-related issues, interpretability of AI models, and regulatory and organizational barriers.

During our interview with CGI, one of the largest IT and business consulting services firms in the world, Diane Gutiw, PhD, VP Global AI Research, CGI, shared with us that the top concerns facing GAI implementation for a healthcare operation are really no different than concerns with coding with java or. NET, "What are you using it for?," she said.

DOI: 10.4324/9781003665434-6

Dr. Gutiw then went on to say that the main issues right now can be put under the umbrella of five principles:

1. **Privacy/Security** – making sure information that is sensitive is well protected and access to PII is restricted to need to know and approved depending on the data and context.
2. **Reliability** – the AI output must be correct, reliable, relevant, complete to be trusted. Adoption will not be possible without these things in healthcare.
3. **Transparency** – to be trusted the source of information and AI-generated content and answers must be clear.
4. **Governance** – there needs to be governance to decide where to invest in AI, when to use AI, and how to scale solutions.
5. **Beneficence** – the potential of unintended harm needs to be protected to ensure that people or populations are not unintentionally targeted or called out from use of AI

Each category intersects with the others in ways that make the implementation of GAI both demanding and fraught with risk. This chapter explores these challenges in depth. Our goal is not simply to itemize the hurdles but to contextualize them for readers seeking to understand and hopefully help overcome them and usher in the promises of the responsible adoption of GAI in healthcare.

"Because GenAI is relatively new to healthcare, unanticipated surprises are to be expected. Only a handful of organizations have even a year or two of real-world experience, so many long-term best practices remain unproven. Moreover, inconsistent EHR data remains a significant barrier: data integrity must be addressed so GenAI can perform reliably. Finally, the regulatory environment is evolving quickly. Balancing state and federal mandates, ensuring responsible use of AI, and navigating unclear compliance standards will likely be time-consuming and complex," Dr. Priti Patel, Chief Medical Information Officer, John Muir Health System

Technical Hurdles and Infrastructure Limitations

Healthcare institutions span a broad spectrum of sizes and specialties, each with its own existing infrastructure, budget constraints, and resource availability. While some large, research-oriented hospitals boast high-performance computing clusters and advanced digital infrastructures, many smaller clinics or public health institutions still rely on outdated or legacy systems.

Introducing GAI into this uneven landscape presents a variety of technical challenges.

The Need for High-Performance Computing

One of the major hurdles involves having adequate computing resources to train or deploy large language models and other generative algorithms. GAI models typically involve billions of parameters and require enormous computational power to run efficiently. Although cloud-based solutions have made it easier to outsource some of this computational load, the cost of scalable cloud computing can be prohibitive for smaller institutions. Furthermore, data transfer times can be significant if large volumes of patient data need to be moved to cloud-based systems. For example, a hospital in a rural area may not have the robust internet connectivity required to push or pull large datasets quickly, making real-time or near-real-time GAI applications impractical.

Power Requirements and Energy Constraints

Beyond computing power, there is a very real challenge concerning **energy consumption**. Modern AI training and inference workloads can be extremely electricity-intensive, requiring stable and abundant power sources to operate large clusters of GPUs, TPUs, or other specialized hardware. This issue is especially pronounced in regions with antiquated or limited power infrastructure, such as parts of the developing world or rural areas in developed countries. Frequent brownouts or unstable power grids can undermine the reliability and accuracy of AI processes, particularly those that must run continuously, such as real-time patient monitoring or clinical decision support systems.

Even for well-resourced institutions, the cost of electricity to run advanced AI models at scale can become substantial. As AI adoption grows within a healthcare network, the power draw for server rooms or dedicated AI hardware may far exceed previous baselines. This spike in energy consumption not only raises operational costs but also poses environmental concerns related to carbon emissions. Therefore, when planning for GAI implementation, healthcare organizations must take into account **both** the cost and environmental footprint of maintaining the necessary energy infrastructure.

In some low-resource settings, the **lack of reliable power** can be a dealbreaker for deploying advanced AI solutions altogether, as hospital administrators may prioritize power for critical medical equipment, such as ventilators or surgical lights. A prospective GAI system might be seen as non-essential if it cannot operate without risking disruptions to life-critical devices. To address these issues, some technology providers and global health initiatives are exploring more energy-efficient AI architectures, using techniques such as model compression and edge computing. However, these innovations are not yet widespread, and the need for stable, plentiful electricity remains a stumbling block for broad GAI adoption, particularly where it could arguably have the greatest impact on patient care.

Legacy Systems and Interoperability

The fragmented nature of healthcare IT systems presents another significant challenge. Many electronic health record (EHR) systems were developed with limited interoperability in mind, often creating data "silos" that are difficult to integrate. GAI tools, to be effective, typically require seamless access to multiple data streams, from EHR data to imaging data to lab results. If these data streams cannot be integrated due to proprietary data formats, security restrictions, or outdated protocols, the potential impact of GAI is greatly reduced. For instance, a new generative model for radiology might require both X-ray images and textual clinical notes to generate meaningful diagnostic suggestions. However, if these data reside in separate systems that do not communicate or if exporting them requires burdensome manual processes, the model's practical utility diminishes.

Data Storage and Management

Storing and managing the vast quantities of data needed for GAI poses a further infrastructure-related challenge. For many forms of generative modeling, such as those producing synthetic patient data to train other AI models, it is critical to maintain large-scale, secure data repositories. These repositories must support rapid read/write operations and robust version control, especially when models are trained iteratively over time. In practice, even well-funded healthcare centers can struggle with the complexity of designing, implementing, and maintaining data warehouses that meet the demanding criteria of GAI systems. Technologies such as Hadoop, NoSQL databases, or specialized data-lake platforms can help, but these solutions often require specialized technical expertise and additional cost.

Talent and Expertise Gap

Even if an organization has adequate computing resources and a modern data infrastructure, success with GAI hinges on specialized talent. Data scientists, machine learning engineers, and clinical informaticians trained in deep learning techniques are in high demand yet short supply. Moreover, an AI solution—generative or otherwise—cannot thrive without oversight from clinical experts who understand the nuances and context of medical data. Hiring or training such interdisciplinary teams is no small feat, and the financial constraints of many healthcare organizations can limit the potential for building robust GAI-based programs.

Hardware and Software Compatibility

Finally, the choice of hardware accelerators (e.g., GPUs vs. TPUs) and the software stack (e.g., TensorFlow, PyTorch) can directly affect both the performance of GAI models and the ease of integration. Many leading-edge AI techniques rely on specialized libraries that may not be fully compatible with older systems. Healthcare organizations face not only the cost of upgrading hardware and software but also the transitional downtime and training required for staff to adapt. Real-world examples include institutions that have tried to implement advanced imaging-based GAI solutions only to discover that their hardware lacked the necessary GPU capabilities. This often leads to unplanned budget requests, project delays, or even project cancellations.

Data Quality and Availability

AI models, especially generative ones, are heavily dependent on the quality and comprehensiveness of their training data. The medical data domain is inherently complex, requiring a wide array of different data types, such as clinical notes, patient histories, diagnostic images, lab results, genomic data, and more. Each of these data types comes with its own set of challenges in terms of collection, labeling, formatting, and integration.

Variability in EHR Data

EHRs form a central source of patient data used to train GAI models. However, EHRs are notorious for their inconsistencies. Different healthcare providers may use different terminologies, coding systems (e.g., ICD-10 vs. SNOMED CT), and data entry methods. Even within a single institution, manual data entry errors, incomplete records, or inconsistent usage of fields can degrade data quality. A GAI model trained on such noisy or incomplete data may exhibit biases or generate unreliable outputs.

Underrepresentation and Bias

Generative models trained on non-representative data risk perpetuating and even amplifying existing biases. This is especially problematic in healthcare, where underrepresentation of certain demographic groups in datasets can lead to systematically poorer performance for those groups. For instance, if a generative model for dermatological diagnostics is trained primarily on images of light-skinned patients, it may fail to accurately identify conditions in darker-skinned populations. This is not a hypothetical scenario; numerous studies have highlighted racial and ethnic disparities in AI-driven diagnostic tools. Ensuring data diversity thus becomes a critical requirement.

Real-world cases have begun to surface. A 2020 study published in the journal *Science* revealed that an AI system used by healthcare providers to predict which patients would benefit from special care was systematically underestimating the needs of Black patients. Although this was not explicitly a GAI model, the principle remains the same: flawed or biased data leads to flawed or biased AI outcomes. The risk is that generative tools, with their capacity for automatically creating content, could unknowingly replicate or even worsen these biases.

Annotated Data Scarcity

In supervised machine learning (and often in GAI that relies on partially supervised techniques), quality annotations from experts—whether radiologists, pathologists, or geneticists—are invaluable. However, expert annotations are time-consuming and expensive. Busy clinicians often do not have the bandwidth to label large datasets, and budgets rarely allow for extensive annotation programs. While GAI can sometimes reduce the requirement for manually labeled data by generating synthetic training examples, the initial model still needs a reliable ground truth. In domains such as oncology, pathology, or cardiology, the absence of large, well-annotated datasets is one of the primary bottlenecks to developing robust GAI solutions.

Privacy and Consent

Collecting high-quality data for GAI is further complicated by privacy concerns and regulatory requirements. Healthcare data is among the most sensitive types of personal data, and regulations like the Health Insurance Portability and Accountability Act (HIPAA) in the US, the General Data Protection Regulation (GDPR) in the European Union, and other similar frameworks globally place stringent restrictions on data sharing and usage. Even though synthetic data generation can, in theory, protect patient privacy by creating anonymized datasets, the process of getting to that stage still requires secure, privacy-compliant environments. In some cases, de-identification is imperfect, raising fears that synthetic data might be reverse-engineered to reveal private patient information. This leads many institutions to err on the side of caution, limiting the scope of data sharing and thereby diminishing data availability for GAI projects.

Data Integration and Federation

A promising avenue to address some of these issues is "federated learning," which enables AI models to be trained on distributed datasets without the data itself leaving local servers. However, implementing federated learning for GAI adds another layer of complexity. Different institutions must maintain compatible systems, training cycles must be carefully orchestrated, and updates need to be shared securely. While this approach could help mitigate privacy concerns and promote data sharing, the complexity of orchestrating such multi-institution collaborations should not be underestimated.

In summary, data quality and availability remain fundamental challenges. Poor or incomplete data can render even the most advanced GAI tools ineffective or harmful, while the difficulty of gathering comprehensive, well-labeled, and representative medical datasets hampers progress. Addressing these issues requires robust data governance frameworks, interdisciplinary collaboration, and innovative technical solutions designed to respect privacy and security needs.

Interpretability of AI Models

Interpretability is crucial in healthcare, where decisions can mean the difference between life and death. GAI models, often built on deep learning architectures such as generative adversarial networks (GANs) or Transformer-based language models, are notoriously opaque. They involve complex, multi-layered networks whose internal decision-making processes are not easily understood even by domain experts.

The Black-Box Problem

Many GAI architectures function as "black boxes," producing outputs, like synthetic patient data, recommended treatments, or generated text, without offering a clear rationale for how they arrived at that conclusion. Clinicians are trained to seek causal or at least evidence-based explanations for medical decisions. Without transparency, it becomes difficult for physicians to trust or act upon GAI-generated suggestions. This lack of interpretability can also create legal liability issues. In the event of an adverse patient outcome, a hospital relying on GAI might struggle to demonstrate the clinical reasoning that led to the decision if it was primarily guided by an opaque algorithm.

The Regulatory Perspective

Regulatory bodies such as the U.S. Food and Drug Administration (FDA) have emphasized the importance of explainability or interpretability in AI-based medical devices. Although guidelines for AI/ML-based Software as a Medical Device (SaMD) are still evolving, there is a growing consensus that interpretability is necessary to ensure patient safety and maintain public trust. This is especially relevant for tools that go beyond mere pattern recognition and venture into generating new content, diagnoses, or treatment recommendations. If the development pipeline cannot demonstrate how data is processed and how outputs are derived, regulatory approval may be delayed or denied.

Techniques for Interpretability

Researchers are actively exploring methods to open the black box of deep learning. These include saliency maps, Layer-wise Relevance Propagation (LRP), Shapley values, and feature attribution methods that aim to show which aspects of the input data most strongly influenced the model's output. For text-based generative models, attention weights can sometimes offer insights into which phrases or tokens were most influential in generating a response. However, these methods have limitations. Saliency maps in medical imaging may highlight regions of a scan that influenced a classification, but they do not necessarily explain "why" the model interprets those pixels as malignant vs. benign. Moreover, interpretability methods often require advanced technical skills to implement and interpret, adding to the resource burden.

Balancing Performance and Interpretability

A critical tension arises between maximizing accuracy and maintaining interpretability. Highly complex models—like large-scale Transformer architectures—may yield extremely accurate results but offer minimal transparency. Conversely, simpler models (e.g., smaller neural networks or traditional statistical models) may be easier to interpret but lack the predictive power needed for advanced tasks such as real-time patient monitoring or sophisticated image synthesis. Healthcare organizations must weigh these trade-offs carefully. In some cases, especially where clinical decisions have serious consequences, a slightly less accurate but more interpretable model might be preferable.

Ethical and Psychological Dimensions

Interpretability has ethical and psychological dimensions as well. Clinicians are more likely to trust and adopt a technology if they understand how it works and why it might fail. Moreover, patients often want to know how a diagnosis was reached. If a GAI tool suggests a particular course of treatment with no interpretable rationale, the patient may be justified in asking, "Why should I trust this recommendation?" This underscores the importance of investing in methods that demystify AI, perhaps through user-friendly interfaces or educational initiatives aimed at both healthcare providers and patients.

In essence, interpretability is not merely a technical challenge but a sociotechnical one that intersects with regulatory, ethical, and cultural considerations in healthcare. Solving the black-box problem will require innovations in model design, enhanced regulatory frameworks, and concerted efforts to build trust among clinicians and patients alike.

Regulatory and Organizational Barriers

Regulations play a critical role in safeguarding patient well-being and maintaining trust in healthcare. While essential, many fear that regulations can pose substantial barriers to the rapid adoption of innovative technologies like GAI. Coupled with organizational inertia and resistance to change, the regulatory environment is a "necessary evil" that could slow down or even stall promising AI initiatives.

FDA Approval Processes for AI-Based Medical Devices

In the US, the FDA has begun implementing frameworks specifically addressing AI/ML-based software, but these are still evolving. This extends to GAI systems that generate or synthesize medical data or offer diagnostic guidance. Although a few AI-based medical devices have received FDA clearance or approval, most rely on more traditional machine-learning approaches (e.g., classification algorithms for medical imaging). GAI tools, with their capacity to produce novel content such as synthetic patient records or predictive analytics, present a new frontier that current regulations are only partially equipped to handle.

Premarket Clearance and Approval

Medical devices that incorporate AI typically undergo either the 510(k) premarket notification process or the more stringent Premarket Approval (PMA) process, depending on the device's risk classification. Demonstrating substantial equivalence to a previously cleared device can be challenging when the core functionality involves generating new content rather than matching a known reference. GAI could, for instance, create synthetic mammogram images to augment training data for breast cancer detection systems. The question remains: how does one prove that these synthetic images are "substantially equivalent" to real mammograms for regulatory purposes? The FDA has begun to offer guidance on "Predetermined Change Control Plans" for AI systems that evolve over time, but generative models add additional complexity by not simply adjusting parameters but actively creating new outputs.

Post-Market Surveillance

Even after receiving clearance or approval, AI-based devices are subject to post-market surveillance to monitor real-world performance. For GAI, tracking performance can be more complicated. If a model continuously learns and updates its parameters or if it generates new synthetic datasets that feed subsequent models, the resulting system's behavior might change over time. Ensuring that these changes do not adversely affect patient safety or device efficacy demands robust monitoring tools and workflows. This can be a tall order for many organizations that do not yet have the infrastructure for continuous validation and monitoring of AI/GAI performance.

Real-World Cases

A notable example of the regulatory pathway for AI is Viz.ai's stroke detection platform, which received FDA clearance through the 510(k) process. Though not generative, it highlights how AI-based tools may receive regulatory blessings. In the future, a GAI solution might similarly analyze imaging data to propose personalized treatment plans or create synthetic training datasets for clinical AI tools. Successfully navigating FDA scrutiny will require these GAI developers to demonstrate safety, efficacy, and interpretability in ways that align with evolving guidelines.

Regulation can be a hurdle to overcome. However, the need for some guidelines and guardrails cannot be understated if we want to ensure fair and ethical use of Gen AI now and in the future. People often think of regulation as a bad thing, and it places a burden on creativity and technical innovation. But, in the real world, particularly as it relates to the large-scale adoption of new tech for the good of all, that is not really the case. Take automobiles, for example. The reason we all own automobiles today and have a wonderful highway infrastructure that can take us anywhere in the world is that we have all literally agreed to the "rules of the road."

That is the thing. From cars to nuclear power or genetic engineering, with every new technology comes this fear of opening a Pandora's Box and unleashing potential hell upon the world. Invariably, however, it is thoughtful regulation that quiets those fears. Boundaries will have to be established, just like they did with CRISPR and gene editing. People thought that was going to bring in the "Brave New World" scenario of "designer babies," but people just put their foot down and said that human gene editing is not going to be allowed, and most countries outlawed it.

Eventually, it is going to have to be the same kind of thing with GAI. We are not sure what it is yet, but some kind of line in the sand will have to be drawn that countries can agree should not be crossed, and this way, bad actors can be prevented without stifling innovation.

Resistance to Change in Healthcare Institutions

Healthcare organizations are complex ecosystems characterized by a strong emphasis on risk management and patient safety. As a result, they often exhibit a conservative mindset when it comes to adopting new technologies. While this caution is understandable—patient safety is paramount—it can also stifle innovation.

Institutional Culture and Workflow Disruption

Introducing GAI tools can disrupt established clinical workflows. For instance, a generative model that proposes diagnoses based on patient data could replace or augment certain steps in the diagnostic process. Clinicians may fear losing control or autonomy, especially if they do not fully understand how the model arrives at its suggestions. Additionally, staff may worry about the time and resources needed to learn new tools, integrate them into existing practices, and address potential errors. Organizational culture often prizes standardized protocols, and any perceived threat to these protocols can trigger resistance.

"I cannot stress enough that we must bring people along for the journey. That means explaining the 'why,' addressing fears about job displacement, and showing team members what's in it for them—whether that's fewer manual tasks, faster access to information, or more meaningful patient interactions.

Technology is the easy part. It's the people and the process that determine whether transformation truly sticks," Crystal Broj, MUSC.

Fear of Liability and Malpractice

Medical liability is a formidable concern. If a GAI-driven decision leads to a misdiagnosis or other adverse patient outcome, who is legally responsible? The clinician who relied on the AI's suggestion, the institution that implemented the technology, or the AI vendor that developed the model? These questions complicate the adoption of novel AI solutions. Although legal frameworks are gradually evolving to address AI-specific concerns, uncertainty about liability can deter healthcare administrators from taking risks on GAI tools.

Budget Constraints and Resource Allocation

Implementing GAI often requires considerable upfront investment in infrastructure, expertise, and training. Healthcare organizations operate under financial constraints, and the return on investment (ROI) for AI initiatives can be difficult to calculate. GAI might reduce some costs, such as by automating certain tasks or reducing diagnostic errors, but these savings may not be realized for years. In many cases, administrators are reluctant to dedicate budgetary resources to a technology whose benefits are not immediately evident.

The Role of Champions and Early Adopters

Despite these challenges, some healthcare institutions have successfully adopted GAI by leveraging visionary leadership and clear value propositions. For example, the Mayo Clinic and the Cleveland Clinic have each invested in AI research centers, forging partnerships with tech companies like Google and IBM to explore generative models for clinical applications. These institutions serve as proving grounds, demonstrating the feasibility and potential ROI of GAI solutions. Their success can inspire other healthcare systems to follow suit, provided they see tangible improvements in patient outcomes and operational efficiency.

Change Management Strategies

Addressing institutional resistance requires a multi-pronged change management strategy. This includes transparent communication about the objectives and limitations of GAI, involving clinicians and nurses early in the design and testing phases, and providing ongoing education and training. It is also essential to set realistic goals and manage expectations. Over-promising the capabilities of GAI can lead to disappointment and backlash when the technology inevitably encounters real-world complexities. By fostering a culture of innovation that respects clinical judgment and patient safety, organizations can gradually integrate GAI into their workflows without triggering excessive pushback.

"It is true that resistance to AI persists," says Vinod Khosla. "Incumbents resist change because they're built to protect the status quo and avoid risk. AI governance, legal concerns, and bureaucratic inertia are good excuses not to take any risks. But in the process, we do much more patient harm at increased costs and withhold due care by omission instead of commission. We need to take some initiative, with appropriate cautions, to reap the benefits of innovation and this once-in-a-lifetime opportunity to dramatically change healthcare for the better."

Interplay of Challenges and Potential Solutions

The challenges described so far do not exist in isolation; they overlap and reinforce one another. For instance, inadequate infrastructure can impede data collection, leading to poor data quality, which then compromises the interpretability and reliability of GAI models. Meanwhile, regulatory uncertainty can exacerbate organizational resistance, making it more difficult to secure the resources needed to address technical and data-related hurdles. This interplay creates a complex web of challenges that must be navigated holistically.

Collaborative Ecosystems

A promising way forward is the creation of collaborative ecosystems involving healthcare providers, technology companies, regulatory bodies, and academic institutions. Collaborative platforms can share not only data but also best practices, lessons learned, and even IT resources. Some leading academic medical centers have started forming consortia aimed at pooling resources for AI/GAI research and development.

Standardization and Common Frameworks

Standards and guidelines play an essential role in reducing uncertainty and streamlining adoption. Initiatives like the Fast Healthcare Interoperability Resources (FHIR) standard from HL7 are already making EHR data more interoperable. Extending such standards to support generative workflows—e.g., standardizing the representation of synthetic data—could further accelerate GAI adoption. Likewise, industry-specific guidelines from professional associations (e.g., the Radiological Society of North America and the American Medical Informatics Association) can offer recommendations on data annotation, privacy, and model interpretability, helping institutions adopt uniform best practices.

Resolving Black Box Issues

A major challenge consistently raised is the "black box" nature of GAI models. Many generative algorithms, particularly large language models and deep neural networks, work through complex, multi-layered processes that even their developers struggle to fully elucidate. This opacity can undermine clinician trust and complicate regulatory approval. In an industry as risk-averse as healthcare, a lack of interpretability becomes a significant barrier to widespread adoption.

Here, technology companies themselves have an especially pivotal role to play. While they naturally want to protect proprietary algorithms and maintain a competitive edge, excessive secrecy can fuel distrust. To overcome this, some GAI vendors have begun embracing "glass box" approaches or at least offering partial transparency into their models. For instance, a model might provide interpretable summaries or "explanations" of how it weighs various input features to arrive at an output. Other firms are exploring methods like attention visualization or saliency mapping, which highlight the data points that most influence the final result. In more advanced scenarios, companies could deliver "explainable AI" toolkits that show how changes to certain inputs impact the GAI's output, helping clinicians better understand the system's internal logic.

Still, not all stakeholders have the same requirements for transparency. For some, a validated performance metric might suffice as long as the model demonstrates robust clinical utility and safety. However, for applications that directly guide patient care, such as recommendations for surgical treatment or dosage, clinicians and regulators often need deeper insight. Hence, a compromise between open and closed architectures could emerge. This middle ground could include independent third-party audits, where recognized experts evaluate a model's architecture and performance without disclosing trade secrets to the broader public. Such audits might become a standard requirement for high-risk GAI applications in healthcare, ensuring patient safety and building trust without disincentivizing innovation.

Alongside these measures for greater transparency, organizations must also monitor and audit GAI performance over time. A model that functions well in one context may degrade when presented with new patient populations, data formats, or clinical conditions. Continuous evaluation and recalibration help catch issues early, such as algorithmic drift or unintentional biases creeping into the system.

Regulatory Sandboxes

Regulatory sandboxes, like those piloted in the financial technology (fintech) sector, could be adapted to healthcare. In a sandbox, companies and institutions can experiment with new technologies under the oversight of regulators but with certain relaxed requirements or temporary exemptions that facilitate innovation. This controlled environment allows for real-world testing of GAI tools while safeguarding patient safety. Lessons learned from sandbox experiments can then inform more permanent regulatory frameworks.

Ongoing Education and Advocacy

Education is perhaps the single most critical factor in overcoming both regulatory and organizational resistance. Clinicians need to understand not only how to operate GAI tools but also the principles behind their operation, enough to form a working mental model. Administrators and policymakers require education on the potential benefits, limitations, and ethical considerations, so they can make informed decisions about resource allocation and policy development. Patient advocacy groups can also play a pivotal role by demanding clarity and transparency about how AI-driven tools make decisions that affect their care.

Fostering Trust through Results

Ultimately, trust in GAI will grow if and when these tools demonstrate tangible improvements in patient outcomes, workflow efficiencies, and cost savings. Early success stories—like using GANs to generate synthetic MRI images for more robust training of diagnostic models—need to be publicized and scrutinized to build confidence. Independent validation studies and peer-reviewed publications can further solidify the credibility of GAI solutions. As trust grows, the barriers—both technical and cultural—may begin to lower.

Case Study: Overcoming Challenges at a Mid-Sized Hospital

To illustrate these challenges and potential mitigations, consider a hypothetical but plausible scenario of a mid-sized hospital (let's call it Riverdale Medical Center) looking to implement a GAI-based tool for generating synthetic patient data to train a sepsis detection model. Riverdale's leadership recognizes that sepsis is a major cause of morbidity and mortality, and an accurate early warning system could save lives.

- **Technical Hurdles**: Riverdale's IT infrastructure consists of older servers and limited GPU capabilities. Even though they considered migrating to a cloud platform, concerns about data privacy and recurring cloud costs gave them pause. Instead, they secured a state grant to upgrade their on-premise data center, ensuring they have a GPU cluster capable of handling GAI training tasks.
- **Data Quality and Availability**: Riverdale's EHR data is fragmented across different departments. A multi-disciplinary team spent six months consolidating and cleaning the data, establishing standardized coding practices for diagnoses, lab values, and patient outcomes. They also partnered with a nearby academic institution that contributed additional de-identified patient datasets from a similar demographic, increasing the size and diversity of their training pool.
- **Interpretability**: To address clinician concerns, the sepsis detection model integrates explainability features, offering a "rationale" dashboard that highlights key lab values, vital signs, and clinical notes. While not a perfect solution, this at least provides clinicians with a sense of why the model might flag a patient as high-risk for sepsis.
- **Regulatory and Organizational Barriers**: Riverdale engaged with their state health department early in the process, clearly outlining the project scope, patient safety protocols, and the benefits of synthetic data. They also set up a hospital-wide committee that included representatives from clinical departments, IT, legal, and risk management. This committee met monthly to discuss progress, review results, and address any regulatory or liability concerns in real-time.

By tackling each challenge in a coordinated manner—securing funding for technical upgrades, cleaning and diversifying data, building interpretability features, and proactively engaging with regulators and stakeholders—Riverdale managed to deploy a pilot GAI system. Early results indicate an improvement in the sepsis early warning system's sensitivity, with fewer false positives than the previous model. While this is just one hypothetical example, it demonstrates how structured planning and collaborative effort can make GAI a reality in healthcare settings that might otherwise struggle with these complex challenges.

In a not-so-fictional example, our own consulting firm, BigRio, developed an LLM-based solution for Vivid Health when they wanted to build a solution for workflow efficiencies that would assist with clinical staff shortages, administrative burden, and the need for patient engagement. We developed an LLM-driven end-to-end solution that today can assess a patient's status on any combination of more than 100 chronic conditions across sixteen specialties, generating personalized care plans at scale in under 30 seconds. That's over 75 million possible care plan combinations in a fraction of the time it typically takes to pull together individualized plans.

Vivid Health's GAI-driven care management platform is currently the most powerful on the market. Its successful development and deployment stand as a testament to GAI's potential to enhance the quality and efficiency of healthcare delivery.

Final Thoughts

GAI offers incredible promises for transforming healthcare, from diagnosing diseases and personalizing treatments to creating synthetic datasets that preserve patient privacy while accelerating research. Yet, the path to widespread adoption is replete with challenges that demand careful navigation. Institutions must grapple with technical infrastructure limitations, data quality and availability, interpretability concerns, and a regulatory landscape that is still evolving. At the same time, organizational barriers—ranging from institutional inertia to fear of liability—can impede adoption even when the technology itself is ready.

At Novo Nordisk, Dr. Alicia Abella leads AI adoption with a disciplined, product management mindset—applying principles she honed at AT&T and Google to ensure AI and GenAI initiatives are purposeful and impactful.

During an interview for an episode of our podcast, *The Big Unlock,* Dr. Abella related how she applies a disciplined product mindset to GenAI implementation, emphasizing that not every problem needs AI, and that user need, business value, and feasibility must come first. She prioritizes AI use cases like knowledge search, market research, and marketing content generation—ensuring each is vetted through rigorous compliance checks. Her close partnership with legal, ethics, and risk teams begins at the ideation stage, allowing innovation to thrive within pharmaceutical regulations. This governance-light, innovation-friendly approach is especially vital in a highly regulated industry like pharma.

Looking ahead, Dr Abella believes the next evolution of GenAI lies at the intersection of intelligent systems and intuitive user experiences. She points to ChatGPT's simplicity as a model for successful adoption, underscoring that usability is as critical as capability. Future GenAI solutions, she suggests, must integrate contextual understanding and mimic aspects of human reasoning to be truly impactful. Drawing inspiration from Star Trek's character Mr. Data, Dr Abella envisions a world where machines enhance human potential without replacing it—striking a thoughtful balance between innovation and humanity.

Getting to such a world will require a concerted and collaborative effort among healthcare providers, regulatory bodies, AI developers, academic researchers, and, perhaps most critically, clinicians and patients. The point is they can be addressed, and that should encourage GAI-centric startups to whom I say, "If GAI and healthcare are your focus, go all in." In fact, we say that startups should focus on solutions to circumvent these challenges. Technical hurdles can be overcome through strategic investments in data centers, cloud computing, and specialized AI talent. Data quality issues can be mitigated by standardizing data collection, embracing federated learning, and ensuring diverse representation in training datasets. Interpretability remains a work in progress, but emerging techniques offer a path toward more transparent AI systems that can be safely and effectively integrated into clinical workflows.

Meanwhile, a forward-looking regulatory approach—potentially aided by initiatives like regulatory sandboxes—can strike a balance between innovation and patient safety. Finally, organizations themselves must cultivate cultures that value evidence-based experimentation, open communication, and continuous education to overcome inertia and apprehension.

The stakes could hardly be higher, as successful implementation of GAI in healthcare has the potential to save lives, reduce costs, and improve patient outcomes on a massive scale. The challenges are daunting but not insurmountable. By learning from early successes and failures, engaging multiple stakeholders, and demonstrating real-world value, generative AI can move from theoretical promise to practical reality.

In the next chapters, we will delve into emerging best practices for implementation, real-world use cases, and visions of the future in which GAI is seamlessly integrated into every layer of healthcare. The journey is just beginning, but the lessons learned from these initial challenges lay the groundwork for a more innovative, equitable, and effective healthcare system for all.

Chapter 7

Integration of GAI into Medical Practice

AI has allowed me, as a physician, to be 100% present for my patients.

Michelle Thompson, DO, Family Medicine Specialist with the University of Pittsburgh Medical Center

As we have seen thus far, generative AI (GAI) stands at the nexus of advanced computational science and healthcare innovation, offering remarkable new capabilities for patient care, research, and operational efficiency. Up to this point in our exploration, we have examined how GAI functions, the benefits it offers to diagnostics and treatment, the ethical and privacy concerns it entails, and the considerable challenges that arise when bringing these advanced systems into clinical environments.

This chapter shifts from identifying potential obstacles to focusing on actionable strategies for integrating GAI into an existing medical practice. By addressing real-world adoption frameworks, training programs, examples of successful startups, and the emerging need for specialized AI leadership roles, we provide a comprehensive and proven roadmap for healthcare institutions aiming to harness GAI's transformative power while avoiding common pitfalls.

When it comes to best practices for integrating Gen AI tools into an existing practice, whether that be an individual doctor's office, a small clinic, or a major hospital network, the same challenge exists, and that is integration with legacy IT, specifically EMR. These days, most practices are using EPIC for EMR/EHR, so let's take EPIC as an example.

DOI: 10.4324/9781003665434-7

EPIC itself has said that the number one inquiry they get coming into customer service right now is how to integrate with GAI. EPIC is quite ubiquitous across the healthcare landscape right now. But, at its core, EPIC is an EMR. It cannot do everything that Gen AI can, but when integrated with Gen AI, you have a powerful combination. Since the EPIC infrastructure is already there in most facilities, the easiest path to integrating GAI is to use something that can work seamlessly with existing EPIC IT.

For instance, with EPIC as the infrastructure base, you may want to now integrate Salesforce, or some other GAI-LLM bases CRM tool, or something like NetSuite for accounting and payroll, or Workday for HR, etc. This has become so part and parcel to GAI integration in healthcare that our own company, BigRio now has a division solely devoted to EPIC implementation and integration with AI.

Strategizing for Successful Adoption

Successful integration of GAI in healthcare does not happen overnight. It demands a series of carefully orchestrated steps that respect the complexity of clinical workflows, the regulatory environment, and the profound responsibility healthcare providers bear toward patient well-being. Although the specifics vary across organizations, certain universal principles underlie a strategic approach to GAI adoption.

One foundational principle is the alignment of AI initiatives with institutional objectives. Healthcare providers typically strive for enhanced patient outcomes, operational efficiency, and compliance with relevant regulations. Any GAI project, whether it involves natural language processing to automate clinical documentation or generative models that synthesize medical images, must align with these objectives to gain traction among stakeholders.

"What we did at Seattle Children's Hospital was take thirty-plus years of valuable clinical data on treating disease in children that was housed in thousands of PDFs and made them instantaneously available leveraging Gen AI," Dr. Zafar Chaudry, SVP, Chief Digital Officer and Chief AI and Information Officer, Seattle Children's.

> We're in beta testing, and it's working very well. We've had fifteen teams of people look at this, and we are already seeing how it is going to revolutionize how quickly care can be provided. It's also revolutionary for training new docs because they're learning and they want to ask a lot of questions, so they can learn about different conditions and how to treat them leveraging GAI.

Leaders like Dr. Chaudry, who champion AI, must clearly articulate how the technology supports broader institutional goals such as reducing readmission rates, improving diagnostic accuracy, or lowering operational costs. This alignment often starts with a thorough needs assessment. Hospital executives or departmental heads must ask, "Where can GAI have the greatest impact?" rather than "What new AI tool is trending in the market?" By framing GAI as a means to address pressing clinical and administrative challenges, healthcare organizations increase the likelihood that staff and administrators will embrace the technology.

Of course, strategy alone cannot overcome ingrained skepticism. Some clinicians may harbor doubts about the reliability and interpretability of GAI tools. Others may question whether a new AI-driven system will increase their daily administrative burden or complicate patient interactions. Addressing these fears requires consistent, transparent communication about what GAI can and cannot do. For instance, if an institution plans to deploy a GAI-enabled clinical decision support tool, clinicians should be involved from the earliest stages of prototype testing. Their feedback on workflow integration, user interface design, and interpretability features will foster a sense of ownership. They are more likely to see GAI as an ally rather than a threat.

Moreover, it helps to identify quick wins that demonstrate tangible benefits early on. For example, a hospital might implement a generative model to automate the creation of discharge summaries, freeing clinicians from hours of repetitive administrative tasks. If clinicians witness improved efficiency without compromises in clinical quality or patient safety, they will be more inclined to trust and champion subsequent GAI deployments. Conversely, launching a large, multi-department initiative without adequately preparing staff and workflows often leads to confusion, resistance, and potential harm. Strategic pacing is essential. Some institutions adopt a phased approach, beginning with pilot programs in one department, such as radiology or pathology, before expanding to other areas. This staged process ensures that lessons learned can inform subsequent, larger-scale rollouts.

Another strategic consideration is the importance of partnering with technology vendors and research institutions. While some large healthcare organizations have in-house data science teams capable of building and maintaining GAI solutions, many others benefit from collaborative efforts. A robust partnership with a reputable AI vendor can accelerate development, ensure regulatory compliance, and provide ongoing support. However, these partnerships must be carefully managed, especially in terms of data sharing and intellectual property. Clear contracts that detail data governance, model ownership, and liability in case of errors can help mitigate potential conflicts. In parallel, collaboration with academic research centers or government agencies can offer additional resources for validation studies, sharing best practices, and even securing grant funding for pilot projects. Each strategic partnership brings different value propositions, and healthcare leaders must weigh these benefits against the need to maintain tight security and patient confidentiality.

Training Programs for Clinicians and Staff

The most sophisticated GAI system in the world will fail to meet its potential if clinicians and support staff do not understand how to use it—or, worse yet, do not trust it. Comprehensive training programs are, therefore, indispensable for successful GAI integration. These programs should not be seen as optional add-ons; instead, they form an integral component of any GAI deployment strategy.

A well-designed training program covers multiple dimensions. On the technical side, clinicians and staff need hands-on experience with the user interfaces of the GAI tools they are expected to use. These sessions should walk participants through real-world clinical scenarios, such as diagnosing a particular condition with the help of a generative model, to illustrate how the AI output should be interpreted and integrated into clinical decision-making. Providing interactive, scenario-based training fosters greater engagement and allows participants to ask targeted questions. This sort of training can also highlight areas where the GAI tool might be weaker or prone to error, encouraging clinicians to keep a critical eye on the system's recommendations.

Beyond the technical "how-to," training programs also need to address the conceptual underpinnings of GAI. While few expect practicing physicians or nurses to become experts in advanced machine learning architectures, basic literacy in how GAI models function is critical for informed usage. If a radiologist understands that a generative adversarial network produces synthetic images by balancing a generator and a discriminator, she may be better equipped to interpret unusual model outputs. Similarly, explaining how certain biases might infiltrate AI models through skewed training data can alert clinicians to the importance of diverse data sets. When medical staff grasp these fundamental principles, they can more effectively scrutinize AI-generated outputs, ask pertinent questions, and help refine the technology.

Institutions also benefit from cross-disciplinary training sessions where clinicians, administrators, IT professionals, and data scientists come together to discuss common goals and concerns. In these forums, data scientists can learn about the daily pressures clinicians face, gaining insight into workflow constraints and real-world obstacles. Conversely, clinicians can become more cognizant of the limitations of current AI methods, learning how best to collaborate with data experts when issues arise. This open communication helps break down the silos that often hinder AI adoption in healthcare. Moreover, by facilitating cross-departmental discussions, administrators can glean valuable feedback on organizational readiness, budget requirements, and potential areas of friction.

To solidify the value of training, healthcare organizations should track and measure their outcomes. For instance, after a round of GAI training, they might assess whether clinicians demonstrate increased proficiency with the new tools via user satisfaction surveys, performance metrics, or follow-up focus groups. Although training requires a substantial time investment, it typically pays dividends in the form of smoother adoption, fewer errors, and a more positive overall attitude toward AI-driven technologies.

Ambient Listening as a Case Study in Successful GAI Implementation

The conceptual shifts described in the previous sections—strategizing for successful adoption and building robust training programs—often come into sharp focus when we look at a concrete example. Ambient listening technology in healthcare epitomizes how a novel AI solution can evolve from an "interesting idea" to a "must-have tool," transforming clinical workflows, influencing hiring decisions, and reshaping how data is captured in real time.

Ambient listening, at its core, uses an AI system—often equipped with natural language processing and generative models—to "listen" to doctor-patient interactions in the background. This system captures the conversation, analyzes relevant clinical details, and automatically generates documentation, such as progress notes or treatment plans, within a patient's electronic health record (EHR). What once seemed futuristic has quickly become a sought-after functionality. Many physicians, especially younger clinicians who grew up in an era of digital integration, now consider the presence of ambient listening tools a crucial factor when deciding where to practice.

The journey from idea to necessity involved several pivotal steps that align closely with the adoption and training insights covered above. Early pilot programs often involved a subset of physicians willing to test AI-driven "listening" systems in real patient encounters. During these pilots, developers and clinicians would refine the user interface and language models, ensuring that the AI accurately captured clinical nuances without intruding on the physician's primary task: attending to the patient. Feedback loops were vital. Clinicians reported on system errors or inaccuracies, prompting iterative improvements in the AI's speech recognition, medical terminology parsing, and context awareness. Over time, these refinements made ambient listening not just tolerable but beneficial, reducing the documentation burden and letting physicians concentrate on patient rapport and clinical thinking.

The key to success was appropriate training. Physicians and their support teams needed to understand how to activate ambient listening, verify the auto-generated notes, and integrate these notes into the EHR without extra steps. Administrators, in turn, needed to see a clear value proposition in the form of fewer transcription costs, reduced physician burnout, or improved documentation accuracy. The synergy between an institution's strategic objectives (streamlined documentation, higher clinician satisfaction) and a well-executed training regimen laid the groundwork for acceptance and eventual enthusiasm.

As momentum grew, word-of-mouth testimonials often played an influential role. Physicians who had used ambient listening in pilot programs reported finishing their shifts with fewer pending charts, a phenomenon sometimes called "pajama time" reduction, referring to the after-hours EHR work many doctors resent. Consequently, newly hired or transitioning clinicians began inquiring whether a prospective employer had implemented ambient listening. What was once a technical curiosity swiftly became a marker of a modern, supportive clinical environment.

Today, a number of vendors provide ambient listening tailored for healthcare settings. Nuance Communications (now a part of Microsoft), known widely for its Dragon medical dictation products, has introduced "Dragon Ambient eXperience (DAX)," leveraging advanced speech recognition to create real-time clinical documentation. Suki AI has developed a voice-enabled digital assistant, also known as a "voice agent," that uses AI to capture and generate notes, while M*Modal (acquired by 3M) offers speech understanding platforms that integrate with major EHR systems. Other players, including Redox, Notable, and various emerging startups, are also innovating in this space. Some solutions lean more on advanced large language models, whereas others emphasize the melding of speech recognition with structured data fields to ensure compliance with coding standards. Regardless of their technical differences, these providers converge on a single value proposition: relieve clinicians of administrative burdens so they can devote more attention to patient care.

The rapid proliferation of ambient listening technology underscores a broader theme in AI adoption for healthcare. Once a solution tangibly alleviates a major pain point, like the endless hours physicians spend on documentation, it can quickly shift from an optional perk to a baseline expectation. This transition is heavily shaped by the clarity of an institution's adoption strategy (making sure the technology fits the organization's broader goals) and the robustness of its training programs (ensuring staff understand how to use and trust the system). In that sense, ambient listening is not just a case study of a single technology's rise; it is a living illustration of how the tenets of strategic alignment, user engagement, and thorough education can transform a clever idea into an indispensable clinical tool.

AI Agents: Revolutionizing Clinical Medicine

The next "big thing" that is liable to go the same route as ambient listening is "Agentic-AI." An AI Agent is a software system powered by artificial intelligence that can perform specific tasks autonomously, making decisions based on data and learning over time; in healthcare, AI agents are utilized to analyze patient data, automate administrative tasks, assist with diagnosis, recommend treatment plans, and generally streamline clinical workflows, allowing healthcare providers to focus on patient care by handling repetitive tasks.

While conventional AI modules typically perform a narrowly defined task, AI Agents behave more like virtual team members who gather insights from multiple data sources, retain contextual information over long interactions, and operate in pursuit of larger objectives such as reducing wait times or optimizing the patient experience.

One key characteristic of AI Agents is autonomy. Rather than merely responding to inputs with canned answers, these agents can make incremental decisions, refine their reasoning as more data comes in, and even proactively identify potential issues that require human intervention. They also demonstrate deeper contextual awareness. An AI Agent assisting in a clinical decision-support scenario can pull a patient's history, current vital signs, and relevant medical literature, then synthesize all of this information to propose diagnostic steps or treatment adjustments.

In today's clinical environment, AI Agents and, in particular, *voice agents* are already being used for tasks like automated triage, scheduling, medication management, and real-time data synthesis. Their ability to parse large datasets swiftly and distill relevant insights has immediate appeal to overburdened care teams, whose time is often split among multiple competing demands. Looking ahead, many experts anticipate that AI Agents will be instrumental in creating an even more GAI-centric healthcare future. Their autonomous, goal-driven nature means they can scale across entire health systems, continually refining their algorithms with real-world feedback. They also open pathways to more personalized patient engagement, whether through interactive symptom checkers, chat-based medication reminders, or wellness-oriented coaching. In essence, AI Agents encapsulate the promise of self-improving, context-sensitive technology that complements clinical expertise while freeing human professionals to focus on complex, high-touch aspects of care.

A recent MIT newsletter says to think of AI agents as AI models "with a script and a purpose." The piece went on to describe the two types of AI agents currently being developed and deployed.

The first, called tool-based agents, can be coached using natural human language, instead of any kind of coding, to complete digital tasks for us. Anthropic released one such voice agent in October, the first from a major AI model-maker. It can translate instructions, i.e., "fill in this form for me," into actions on someone's computer, moving the cursor to open a web browser, navigating to find data on relevant pages, and filling in a form using that data. Salesforce has released its own agent, too, and OpenAI reportedly plans to release one in January.

The other type of agent is called a "simulation agent," and you can think of these as AI models designed to behave like human beings. The first people to work on creating these agents were social science researchers. They wanted to conduct studies that would be expensive, impractical, or unethical to do with real human subjects, so they used AI to simulate subjects instead. This trend particularly picked up with the publication of an oft-cited 2023 paper by Joon Sung Park, a PhD candidate at Stanford, and colleagues called "Generative Agents: Interactive Simulacra of Human Behavior."

Recently, Park and his team published a new paper on arXiv called "Generative Agent Simulations of 1,000 People." In this work, researchers had 1,000 people participate in two-hour interviews with an AI. Shortly after, the team was able to create simulation agents that replicated each participant's values and preferences with stunning accuracy.

There are two really important developments here. First, it's clear that leading AI companies think it's no longer good enough to build dazzling GAI tools; they now have to build agents that can accomplish things for people. Second, it's getting easier than ever to get such AI agents to mimic the behaviors, attitudes, and personalities of real people. What were once two distinct types of agents—simulation agents and tool-based agents—could soon become one thing: AI models that can not only mimic your personality but also act on your behalf.

Research on this is underway. Companies like Tavus are hard at work helping users create "digital twins" of themselves. But the company's CEO, Hassaan Raza, envisions going further, creating AI agents that can take the form of therapists, doctors, and teachers. The following graphic illustrates who can use Agentic Voice Agents and how.

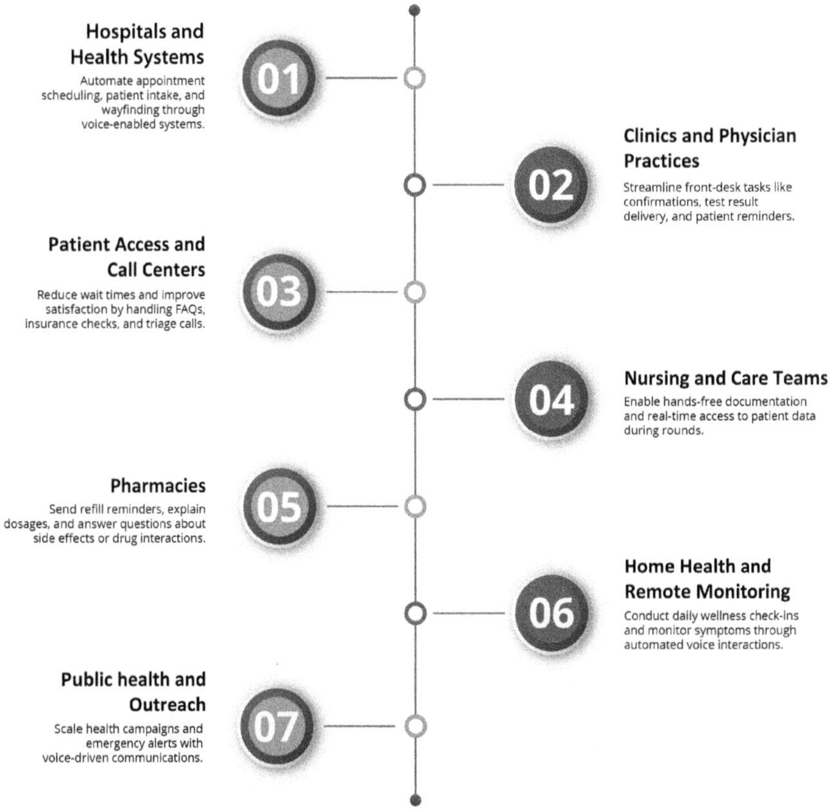

Figure 7.1 Who can use voice agents. This was created by BigRio in-house graphics department.

Successful Startups as Real-World Examples

Figure 7.1 above indicates the kinds of healthcare operations that can benefit from the use of AI voice agents and how. A company known as Mila Health is doing something very interesting on the patient engagement side using GAI and Large Language Models, and it is in the realm of "Agent AI" we discussed earlier in the chapter. They have created a personalized AI healthcare worker that automates patient care before and after visits. Healthcare providers use Mila to autonomously guide patients to manage chronic and other conditions, lowering no-show rates while reducing manual effort. Mila engages patients with empathy, uses behavior change techniques to nudge patients, addresses open-ended questions accurately, learns from past conversations, and motivates them to comply with care plans. Mila integrates with EMRs for seamless provider workflows.

Several provider organizations, including Aayu Clinic, MIMIT Health, and Best Practices Inpatient Care, have already deployed Mila to enhance adherence, save staff time, and improve patient outcomes.

Other than Mila, in the fast-evolving domain of GAI, numerous startups have emerged to fill the gaps between cutting-edge research and practical clinical solutions. Some focus on specialized data sets, such as imaging data for oncology; others develop multi-modal tools that integrate textual, numerical, and image-based information to provide holistic clinical insights. Examining these startups can offer valuable lessons to institutions considering GAI adoption, as these emerging companies often demonstrate agility and innovation.

One noteworthy example is Viz.ai, which has developed AI-driven systems primarily geared toward stroke detection and triage. While Viz.ai's initial offerings centered on more traditional AI algorithms, the company has begun exploring generative approaches to augment diagnostic capabilities. Their stroke detection platform employs advanced imaging analysis to prioritize patients based on the severity of their scans, enabling clinicians to intervene rapidly. Although it is not purely generative, Viz.ai's story illustrates how AI-based medical technologies can navigate regulatory processes and integrate into hospital workflows. The company secured FDA clearance for its algorithms, demonstrating the feasibility of AI—and potentially GAI—in critical, time-sensitive care pathways.

Another relevant startup is BenevolentAI, which has garnered attention for its use of AI in drug discovery. BenevolentAI's platform leverages generative models to identify novel molecular structures that could lead to new medications, drastically reducing the time and cost traditionally associated with pharmaceutical research. Though drug discovery may not seem akin to a typical hospital-based application, the same generative methodologies can be applied to creating synthetic patient data or generating personalized treatment recommendations. BenevolentAI's partnerships with major pharmaceutical companies underscore the shift in the industry toward AI-driven innovation.

In the realm of diagnostics, PathAI stands out for its focus on pathology. While much of its platform utilizes supervised machine learning to assist pathologists in identifying cancerous tissue, the company has begun exploring generative models that can simulate tissue variations for research and training. By collaborating with leading academic institutions, PathAI exemplifies the importance of bridging commercial objectives with rigorous scientific validation. Their success hinges on demonstrating improved diagnostic accuracy without adding burdensome steps to pathologists' workflows—a balance that GAI must also strike.

Beyond these high-profile names, there are numerous smaller startups focusing on narrower but equally vital clinical niches. Some generate synthetic EHR data to train new AI tools without compromising patient privacy. Others build language models that analyze clinical notes and propose potential diagnoses or treatment adjustments based on nuanced textual cues. These startups collectively highlight a pattern: success often requires a deep understanding of clinical workflows, a willingness to iterate and refine algorithms, and a keen eye toward regulatory compliance. Their experiences also illustrate that early adoption of AI tools can yield competitive advantages for healthcare institutions, as well as improve patient care when done responsibly and ethically.

Education Initiatives for Medical Professionals

While training programs are often institution-specific, broader educational initiatives for medical professionals can elevate the baseline AI literacy across the entire field. These initiatives may be spearheaded by professional associations, academic institutions, or even government agencies seeking to modernize healthcare delivery and research.

In many ways, healthcare professionals are being asked to add an additional dimension to their already extensive education. It is one thing to grasp medical knowledge in physiology, pharmacology, and surgical techniques; it is quite another to incorporate fundamental concepts of machine learning, data governance, and technology ethics into daily practice. Recognizing this gap, some medical schools are starting to offer dedicated modules on AI, data science, and digital health, ensuring that the next generation of physicians is better equipped to work with advanced technologies. These courses can offer hands-on tutorials, enabling students to experiment with AI tools—both generative and non-generative—under expert supervision.

Professional organizations have likewise begun to offer AI certification programs or specialized workshops. For instance, the American College of Radiology (ACR) has run an educational series that introduces radiologists to the basics of AI and explores how emerging algorithms can augment diagnostic accuracy. Although these initiatives often focus on the technical side, the best programs also address ethical considerations, emphasizing the importance of validating AI models against bias and ensuring they serve diverse patient populations. More recently, some of these educational efforts have pivoted specifically toward generative models, discussing how synthetic image generation might improve training sets for rare conditions or how large language models can automate the drafting of clinical reports.

Continuing Medical Education (CME) credits provide another pathway to broaden AI competencies among practicing clinicians. By integrating GAI-related courses into CME requirements, healthcare professionals are incentivized to remain current with technological advancements. An internist who must fulfill a certain number of CME hours annually might choose to enroll in a module titled "Generative AI in Chronic Disease Management," learning about how GPT-like models could help identify unrecognized comorbidities. As these CME offerings become more widespread and sophisticated, the baseline technological fluency among healthcare professionals will likely rise.

All of these educational efforts serve to counter the narrative that AI is a black-box technology meant for data scientists alone. By weaving AI concepts into medical education at multiple levels—undergraduate, postgraduate, and continuing education—institutions lay the groundwork for a future workforce that is not only adept at using GAI tools but also capable of critically evaluating them. They nurture a generation of clinicians who can question AI outputs in a constructive manner, partner with AI developers to refine algorithms, and ensure that these tools remain attuned to clinical realities.

Avoiding the Pitfalls: Implementation Do's and Don'ts

Despite the promising horizon of GAI in healthcare, numerous pitfalls can derail even the most well-intentioned implementation. From our earlier chapters, we have already encountered issues such as biases in training data, lack of interpretability, and infrastructure limitations. Here, we revisit some of these concerns but also expand on practical "dos and don'ts" that can steer institutions away from avoidable mistakes.

An essential principle is to engage in transparent communication. When rolling out a new GAI-based diagnostic tool, administrators should explicitly explain the system's purpose, its validation process, and any known limitations. This means being upfront about metrics like sensitivity, specificity, and potential error rates. Clinicians who are blindsided by an AI tool's shortcomings may lose trust altogether, souring them on future deployments. Equally important is involving stakeholders, including front-line nurses, technicians, and even patients, in the discussion. Their insights can highlight overlooked challenges that might surface during everyday clinical use.

A complementary recommendation is not to assume that high accuracy in a research setting automatically translates to success in a real-world clinical environment. Controlled pilot projects are a cornerstone of cautious, responsible GAI implementation. Institutions might test a GAI-based recommendation system on a small cohort of patients or in a single department, gathering comprehensive feedback before scaling. Rushing to a full-scale launch often magnifies minor oversights into major disruptions. By contrast, iterative piloting allows for refinement and fosters gradual acceptance among healthcare staff.

Another "do" is to align GAI projects with ethical and regulatory standards from the outset. Healthcare organizations should not treat regulatory compliance as an afterthought or a box-checking exercise. Rather, compliance with bodies like the FDA or EMA, as well as adherence to frameworks like HIPAA or GDPR, should be integrated into the development and validation lifecycle of any GAI application. Clinicians, legal experts, data scientists, and compliance officers all have a role to play in ensuring that the GAI tool meets or exceeds regulatory requirements and upholds patient privacy and safety.

Conversely, a critical "don't" is to disregard the risk of algorithmic bias. Institutions that do not regularly audit the performance of GAI tools across demographic groups, disease variations, and care settings may unwittingly embed inequalities into their patient care pathways. The burden is on those deploying the AI, not the patients, to verify that it is free from systemic biases. Regular audits, external validations, and periodic recalibration of models help mitigate this risk, ensuring that the GAI system remains fair, equitable, and clinically accurate.

Finally, organizations should be cautious about over-reliance on GAI. While these tools can dramatically augment human capabilities, they are not infallible. Clinical decisions ultimately rest with human practitioners, who must consider patient history, lifestyle factors, and the intangible nuances that AI might miss. Over-dependence on AI recommendations, without proper clinical oversight, can lead to diagnostic oversights and ethical dilemmas. A well-designed GAI system is best viewed as an integral part of a larger ecosystem, complementing rather than replacing the expertise and empathy clinicians bring to patient care.

The Role of the Chief AI Officer (CAIO)

As GAI deployments become more prevalent and complex, many healthcare organizations find themselves in need of specialized leadership to oversee AI strategy, governance, and implementation. Enter the Chief AI Officer (CAIO)—a relatively new role but one that is rapidly gaining traction. The CAIO acts as an executive champion for AI-driven initiatives, bridging technical teams, clinical stakeholders, and the C-suite to ensure that AI deployments are both safe and aligned with organizational objectives.

A CAIO's responsibilities typically encompass several domains. One is **strategic vision**: the CAIO collaborates with senior executives to identify high-impact use cases for GAI, such as improving oncology diagnostics, reducing readmissions, or personalizing patient education. By working closely with department heads, the CAIO can determine which projects merit immediate investment based on factors like potential patient outcomes, operational efficiency gains, and cost-effectiveness. Another domain is **technology governance**: the CAIO helps establish best practices for data collection, model validation, and continuous monitoring, ensuring that GAI systems remain compliant with healthcare regulations and institutional policies. This governance framework sets clear expectations for AI usage, delineates lines of accountability, and clarifies how the institution handles system failures or liabilities.

Additionally, the CAIO plays a pivotal role in **fostering organizational culture**. AI-related skepticism often arises from a lack of understanding or fear that AI may replace human roles. A capable CAIO addresses these concerns by advocating for AI literacy, facilitating collaborative pilot projects, and highlighting success stories that demonstrate how AI can empower rather than supplant clinicians. By encouraging a spirit of learning and experimentation, the CAIO helps ease the cultural barriers that frequently impede AI adoption.

An often overlooked aspect of the CAIO's job is **resource allocation**. AI projects can be expensive, requiring investments in computing infrastructure, data storage, specialized talent, and possibly external vendor partnerships. A CAIO who is well-versed in both finance and technology can make informed decisions about how to allocate limited resources effectively. For instance, they may opt for cloud-based solutions in certain scenarios while prioritizing on-premise GPU clusters for other tasks that demand higher security. Likewise, the CAIO can guide the organization in determining when it makes sense to hire in-house data scientists versus partnering with academic institutions or vendors.

Not every healthcare organization will require a formal CAIO. Smaller institutions might appoint an existing executive (such as a Chief Technology Officer or Chief Medical Information Officer) to oversee AI-related initiatives, especially if the scope is limited to a few targeted applications. However, for large hospital systems, research institutes, or healthcare networks with ambitious AI roadmaps, appointing a CAIO can streamline the adoption process and amplify the impact of GAI tools. Indeed, some progressive institutions have already created AI leadership roles, recognizing that coordinating AI initiatives demands a dedicated expert who combines knowledge of clinical care, data science, and strategic management.

Concluding Thoughts and a Look Ahead

Integrating GAI into medical practice represents one of the most significant shifts in modern healthcare, potentially rivaling the advent of antibiotics or imaging technologies in its transformative impact. Yet, as with any paradigm shift, success depends on more than just the technology's raw capabilities. It hinges on meticulously planned strategies that align with institutional objectives, robust training programs that cultivate AI literacy among clinicians and staff, and a deep-seated commitment to ethical and regulatory standards. Real-world examples from successful startups illustrate the tangible benefits of GAI, from accelerated drug discovery to improved diagnostic workflows. These case studies also underscore the necessity of careful deployment, nuanced validation, and constant iteration.

Education initiatives play an equally critical role, ensuring that AI does not remain the domain of data scientists alone. When nurses, physicians, pharmacists, and administrators understand the mechanics and limitations of AI, they become empowered participants in its deployment rather than passive recipients of black-box solutions. This elevation of collective AI literacy can stimulate more informed discussions around issues like bias, interpretability, and patient trust. In the end, an educated clinical workforce is perhaps the single most important factor in turning GAI's promise into a sustainable reality.

Along the way, pitfalls abound, and the history of technology adoption in healthcare is replete with cautionary tales of overhyped software that failed to deliver. By proactively identifying potential pitfalls—lack of transparency, insufficient pilot testing, regulatory non-compliance, or algorithmic bias—healthcare organizations can avert costly missteps. Each step in the GAI implementation journey, from the earliest feasibility study to the final system-wide rollout, should be informed by rigorous evaluation and open communication with all stakeholders.

Finally, as GAI initiatives scale, the question of leadership becomes ever more pressing. The creation of a CAIO role in larger healthcare organizations reflects the growing recognition that AI is not just another IT project but a transformative engine that can reshape clinical practice, research, and administration. Whether or not an institution adopts the CAIO model, it must ensure that AI governance is thoughtfully structured, that responsibilities are clearly delineated, and that there is a perpetual dialogue between clinicians and technologists.

Looking ahead, the integration of GAI into medical practice will likely accelerate as the technology matures and success stories proliferate. We may soon see generative models that not only aid in diagnoses but also craft individualized patient education materials, design novel treatment pathways, or facilitate real-time monitoring of disease progression. These advancements will undoubtedly spark new ethical, legal, and practical challenges, necessitating a continual evolution of regulatory frameworks and professional standards. Yet the overall trajectory is difficult to dispute: GAI is poised to become an indispensable tool in the healthcare toolkit, reshaping the fundamentals of patient care, medical research, and operational efficiency in ways we are only beginning to fathom.

In the next chapters, we will continue this journey by examining how to measure and demonstrate the impact of GAI, exploring success metrics and potential economic models, and envisioning the broader future of healthcare as AI becomes more deeply integrated into everyday practice. But for now, suffice it to say that the roadmap for GAI adoption is steadily coming into focus. Institutions that proceed with clear-eyed strategies, robust training, ethical vigilance, and the right leadership in place will be well-positioned to reap the benefits of this transformative technology while safeguarding the trust and well-being of the patients they serve.

Chapter 8

Impact on Healthcare Delivery

The greatest opportunity offered by AI is not reducing errors or workloads, or even curing cancer: it is the opportunity to restore the precious and time-honored connection and trust.

Eric Topol, Founder of the Scripps Research Translational Institute, on AI in Healthcare

Gen AI has begun to reshape the contours of healthcare delivery. In the earlier chapters of this book, we explored foundational concepts, ethical considerations, and the logistics of implementation. We also discussed training needs, regulatory hurdles, and the emergence of specialized roles for overseeing AI initiatives. We also looked at a snapshot of how Gen AI is transforming the typical visit to a doctor's office.

Now, it is time to examine how Gen AI's impact extends beyond theoretical applications and day-to-day clinical realities and take a deeper dive into the overall environment and economics of care. The contemporary healthcare landscape is under immense pressure to diagnose illnesses more swiftly, tailor treatment more precisely, and optimize costs without compromising quality. Faced with these challenges, Gen AI emerges not just as an innovation but as a catalyst poised to change how clinical decisions are made, how resources are allocated, and how economic sustainability is pursued and achieved.

As Vinod Khosla expressed so well in our talk, "Healthcare is broken today in many ways - from lack of adequate care, to lack of accessibility, to physician

DOI: 10.4324/9781003665434-8

burnout. AI can and will change this all for the better. In my 2016 piece, '20% Doctor Included,' I imagined a twenty five year transition in medicine driven by AI. The change I envisioned is happening faster and in a bigger way, creating a massive opportunity for healthcare players."

Enhancements in Diagnosis, Treatment, and Patient Outcomes

In any discussion of AI's impact on healthcare, diagnosis, and treatment often take center stage. The speed and accuracy of diagnosis are pivotal determinants of a patient's prognosis. Early identification of a complex condition can quite literally mean the difference between a manageable health episode and a life-threatening crisis. Historically, doctors have relied on their clinical expertise, peer-reviewed literature, and a range of diagnostic tests to arrive at a conclusion. While this approach has served as the backbone of modern medicine, it also comes with human limitations. High patient volumes, administrative burdens, and the sheer volume of medical knowledge expanding each year can strain clinicians' ability to maintain consistently high standards of diagnostic accuracy. When these complexities collide, the margin for error can widen, and that is precisely where Gen AI can offer valuable reinforcement.

One core strength of Gen AI lies in its ability to synthesize diverse data sources into an integrated view. Hospital electronic health records, imaging data, lab test results, and even continuous streams of patient-generated data from wearable devices can be swiftly integrated. While traditional analytics might struggle to discern subtle correlations, generative models can detect patterns that escape the naked eye. This process goes beyond rote data-matching; Gen AI can generate hypothesized scenarios or synthetic patient profiles to stress-test existing diagnostic pathways. It can propose differential diagnoses grounded in real-world data patterns that human practitioners might find difficult to recall, especially in the hustle of day-to-day clinical practice.

Medical professionals who have incorporated Gen AI into their diagnostic workflows have reported a higher degree of confidence when dealing with unusual presentations of diseases. A physician might, for instance, encounter a patient with a rare autoimmune disorder. By consulting a Gen AI model trained on a large, diverse dataset, including examples of rare presentations or comorbidities, the physician can consider possible diagnoses that might otherwise be overlooked. This does not diminish the importance of clinical intuition. Rather, Gen AI augments clinical reasoning by ensuring that atypical yet critical possibilities remain on the differential radar. The immediate impact manifests in more accurate referrals to specialists, swifter confirmations of suspected pathologies, and potentially fewer misdiagnoses, leading to costly or harmful interventions.

Treatment planning has also witnessed transformations due to Gen AI. Beyond standard predictive models that might suggest the most appropriate drug dosage, Gen AI techniques enable dynamic treatment simulations that can account for variations in patient physiology. A generative model might, for instance, forecast how a patient with renal insufficiency might metabolize a particular chemotherapy regimen differently from a patient with normal renal function. By generating these predictive scenarios, the model gives oncologists and pharmacists a clearer picture of how to fine-tune treatment for maximal efficacy and minimal side effects. This level of personalization is especially potent in fields where disease heterogeneity is significant, such as oncology, where tumors with the same clinical label can vary enormously in their molecular makeup and growth patterns.

Although real-world studies of these applications are ongoing, preliminary evidence indicates improvements in patient outcomes. In cardiology, for example, patients with suspected heart failure can be triaged more efficiently when a Gen AI tool swiftly parses echocardiogram images and correlates them with clinical notes. The result could be the early prescription of life-saving medications. Similar benefits have been observed in diabetic care, where continuous glucose monitoring data integrated with personalized nutritional and lifestyle recommendations enhances glycemic control over time. In these settings, enhancements in diagnosis and treatment converge in a meaningful way: earlier detection of complications, better-tailored interventions, and higher rates of patient adherence to therapy. The downstream effect is a tangible improvement in patient outcomes, measured by reduced mortality, lower readmission rates, and improved quality of life for those with chronic conditions.

Despite these promising results, challenges remain. Clinicians may still harbor doubts about the "black box" nature of many deep learning models, which can generate sophisticated outputs without a straightforward explanation. Regulatory guidelines for AI-driven diagnostic decisions are evolving, and reimbursements for AI-guided procedures may not always align with the cost of adopting Gen AI solutions. Yet, these obstacles do not overshadow the breakthroughs. Instead, they emphasize the importance of continued refinement of Gen AI systems, ongoing clinical validation studies, and thoughtful regulatory frameworks. As more success stories accumulate and as the broader ecosystem adapts to the new technology, the likelihood grows that Gen AI will become a foundational element in routine diagnosis, treatment, and patient management.

Early Detection of Diseases through AI-Driven Screening

While the pursuit of accuracy in diagnosis is important, an equally critical dimension of patient care is the timing of that diagnosis. Catching a disease at an early stage can avert complications, reduce treatment costs, and, in many instances, save lives. For decades, public health campaigns have advocated for screening measures—mammograms for breast cancer, colonoscopies for colorectal cancer, and various forms of genetic testing—precisely because early detection correlates so strongly with improved outcomes. Yet, screening programs, especially on a population-wide scale, have long grappled with issues of cost, accessibility, and accuracy. False positives lead to unnecessary worry and interventions, while false negatives can lull patients into a dangerous sense of security. Gen AI has the potential to reshape this landscape, offering the promise of more precise and comprehensive screenings at scale.

One way AI-driven screening improves early detection is through image-based diagnostics, particularly in fields like radiology and dermatology. Traditional imaging systems rely on a radiologist's skill and experience to interpret subtle indicators. By contrast, Gen AI can analyze massive archives of imaging data to identify faint signals that might point to the incipient stages of disease. In mammography, for example, models can now identify minute calcifications or irregularities that even trained eyes might overlook on a busy day. This automated scanning, followed by a second read from a radiologist, often yields a synergy greater than either approach alone. Studies in academic medical centers have begun to report that AI-assisted mammograms can detect cancers at earlier stages with fewer false positives, thereby improving both patient survival rates and patient experience.

Another notable area is lung cancer screening, which traditionally depends on low-dose CT scans for high-risk populations such as heavy smokers. Here, Gen AI can flag suspicious nodules in their earliest, most subtle manifestations. In a field where any delay in detection can be the difference between a localized lesion and metastatic disease, the capacity to spot early signs is a game-changer. Once flagged, patients can undergo follow-up imaging or biopsy sooner, potentially leading to treatment before the disease gains momentum.

Outside of imaging, AI-driven screening has also expanded into computational pathology, where Gen AI examines digital slides for early markers of diseases like prostate cancer or melanoma. Pathologists, like radiologists, can experience fatigue when reviewing hundreds or thousands of slides. Gen AI never tires, and its algorithms can be fine-tuned to detect morphological features consistent with early stage pathology. While no algorithm is perfect, the combination of human expertise and AI vigilance significantly amplifies the likelihood of catching disease early.

There is a particularly exciting frontier in leveraging Gen AI for early detection of diseases that are notoriously challenging to diagnose, including neurodegenerative disorders like Alzheimer's. Machine learning research groups are now developing generative models that analyze subtle changes in brain scans, cerebrospinal fluid biomarkers, or even linguistic and behavioral patterns in patients' daily communications. If clinicians can reliably identify early cognitive decline or subtle neurological anomalies years before classical symptoms manifest, treatment and lifestyle interventions could be introduced at a far earlier juncture. This proactive stance could radically shift the paradigm in conditions that currently have limited treatment options once symptoms become obvious.

These strides in early detection, promising as they are, rest on critical considerations. Ensuring the diversity and representativeness of training datasets remains paramount, lest screening systems fail to perform well among underrepresented populations. Additionally, the logistical challenge of rolling out AI-driven screening programs at scale should not be underestimated. Hospitals and clinics need both the computational infrastructure and the staff training to interpret AI results and manage subsequent steps in diagnosis and care. Nonetheless, AI-driven screening stands as a powerful illustration of how Gen AI is not merely increasing accuracy at the point of care but also moving upstream to identify problems before they escalate, thereby contributing to a more preventive, patient-centered model of healthcare delivery.

Personalized Treatment Plans Based on AI Analysis

Precision medicine has long been a buzzword in healthcare, championed by clinicians, researchers, and policymakers for its promise of matching treatments to each patient's unique genetic makeup, lifestyle, and disease profile. That vision, while compelling, can be extremely complicated to implement in practice. Even the best-equipped hospitals struggle to manage the multitude of variables that constitute a patient's clinical background: genomic data, imaging reports, comorbid conditions, social determinants of health, and real-time vital signs, to name just a few. Gen AI offers a new framework for handling these challenges, allowing for the possibility of highly personalized treatments that reflect the complexity of human biology.

The mechanism by which Gen AI facilitates this level of personalization is multifaceted. On the one hand, generative models can draw upon extensive patient databases, comprising tens or hundreds of thousands of cases, to identify nuanced predictors for treatment success or failure. An oncologist, for instance, might wish to determine which chemotherapy regimen will be most effective for a patient based on the tumor's genomic mutations and the patient's overall health profile. Rather than relying solely on generalized clinical trial data that might not perfectly match that patient's demographic or genetic background, the AI can distill patterns from a vast dataset of patients with similar traits. It can then propose multiple possible treatment paths, highlighting the probable outcomes and side effect profiles associated with each path.

Another essential element of personalized treatment is the continuous monitoring of patients' responses. Gen AI can track patient progress in near real-time if integrated with hospital EHRs or wearable devices. Changes in blood pressure, heart rate variability, lab results, or even textual notes from the patient describing side effects can feed back into the model, prompting adjustments to the treatment plan. This feedback loop embodies the principles of adaptive therapy, where treatment evolves alongside the patient's response rather than following a one-size-fits-all protocol. Imagine a patient with metastatic breast cancer who experiences significant toxicity from a first-line therapy; a generative model might recommend a dose adjustment or propose a second-line therapy that shares a similar mechanism but has a different toxicity profile tailored to the patient's existing comorbidities.

For example, "CGI's OMNI360 AI Assistant can extract relevant information from the patient history, including texts, documentation, imaging, and summary notes which allows the attending physician to interrogate the data and immediately learn more about the patient's health journey to date," explains Ben Goldberg, Global Health Sector Lead, CGI

But what makes solutions like this "next level" beyond first-generation ambient listening tools is solutions like CGI's AI Assistant understand context and the relationships within the data, to accurately respond to a variety of inquiries.

> For instance, a physician may want to learn how balanced the patient's diabetes has been over the past year, said Goldberg. "With a simple conversational prompt, the OMNI360 AI Assistant reviews the patient's medical records, including blood tests measuring glucose and creatinine levels, weight changes, previous diagnoses, and any other event in the clinical history related to diabetes. The results include a concise response, including easily accessible links citing the original medical records.

In many ways, this adaptability exemplifies the synergy between Gen AI and human oversight. The AI can propose alterations at a granularity and speed that human clinicians cannot realistically match, especially when juggling large patient loads. At the same time, the final decision rests with medical professionals who interpret the AI's suggestions in light of clinical judgment, patient preferences, and the intangible nuances of real-world care. By fostering this human-machine collaboration, healthcare delivery evolves from a standard set of protocols to a more dynamic, data-driven model where each patient is, in effect, treated as a unique scenario worthy of customized strategies.

Personalized treatments driven by Gen AI have also begun to show early promise in chronic disease management, where conditions like diabetes or heart failure require continuous fine-tuning of medications and lifestyle interventions. Models can track a patient's glucose levels or ejection fraction over time, propose modifications to medication dosages, or suggest intervals for routine tests. For patients dealing with complex, multi-system conditions, AI's ability to integrate myriad data types—nutrition logs, exercise patterns, medication adherence metrics, lab values—can unearth correlations that point to more refined interventions. It may be that a certain subset of patients with hypertension responds better to a specific class of blood pressure medication when combined with a dietary approach rich in particular micronutrients. Identifying such subgroups and the treatments that benefit them is precisely the realm where Gen AI excels.

Nonetheless, the journey toward fully realized personalized medicine is hardly straightforward. On the technological front, maintaining robust and secure data pipelines remains a prerequisite for enabling the sophisticated analytics needed for real-time treatment guidance. On the ethical front, questions arise about how best to manage patient consent when AI-driven personalization relies on aggregated data from countless other patients. On the clinical front, acceptance from physicians requires that AI proposals are presented in interpretable, user-friendly interfaces and accompanied by transparent rationales for the recommendations given. Each of these facets requires attention if personalized treatments are to progress beyond experimental pilot projects into the mainstream of everyday care. The progress so far suggests, however, that these hurdles—while significant—are surmountable and that Gen AI is well-positioned to spearhead a new era of hyper-individualized healthcare.

Economic Gains: Potential Cost Savings and Efficiency Gains

While improving patient outcomes is the primary aim of any medical innovation, the economic implications of Gen AI adoption are also impossible to ignore. Healthcare systems worldwide, whether publicly or privately funded, grapple with the twin imperatives of cost containment and quality maintenance.

Implementing new technology typically raises questions about return on investment, potential disruptions to workflow, and overall sustainability. Gen AI, if deployed thoughtfully, has the potential to address several of these concerns by streamlining clinical processes, optimizing resource allocation, and reducing inefficiencies that pervade modern healthcare.

An area of particular concern is revenue cycle management (RCM). RCM in healthcare refers to the comprehensive process of managing all financial aspects of patient care, from the initial appointment to the final payment. It involves a series of coordinated steps to ensure that healthcare providers receive timely and accurate reimbursement for the services they provide.

RCM in healthcare still requires multiple manual steps, which lead to significant delays in patient care, loss of revenue for healthcare systems, and burnout amongst clinicians. There are many steps in RCM that can be automated and simplified using generative AI (GAI). Pre-authorization by insurance for delivery of clinical care is one of these key areas that has been highlighted and advocated for change by organizations such as the American Medical Association (AMA). Prior authorization processes have relied heavily on human intervention, including reviewing detailed medical histories, interpreting insurance requirements, and communicating between payers and providers. This labor-intensive approach is time-consuming and prone to error, especially as insurance policies grow increasingly complex and diverse. Inappropriate delays and denials of care have been a major area of public and governmental concern. AI automation has often been recommended as an elegant solution to prevent such denials. Also, pre-authorization and electronic health record management rank as the top reasons for burnout amongst clinicians. Despite recommendations to leverage GAI-driven portals for health information exchange amongst healthcare providers and insurance companies, only a few solutions have been built to facilitate it.

"Applying GAI across these steps will streamline workflows, reduce administrative burdens, and accelerate time to care for patients. Tasks such as data collection, sorting, and categorization have now been made easier while handling multiple sources of data, including paper, electronic records, or electronic health records. This automation removes a significant number of delays and loss of information in the key first step of data collection and preprocessing. With GAI, extraction of key data elements related to patient information and their insurance detail verification has been simplified. Verification and validation of insurance coverage for requested clinical care episodes can then be automated to expedite the processing of the coverage request," said Dr. Piyush Mathur, Staff Anesthesiologist and Critical Care Physician, Cleveland Clinic/Brain X.

In our interview with Dr. Mathur, he added, "Soon, the AI algorithms will predict whether a request is likely to be approved or denied based on historical patterns, payer-specific requirements, and patient-specific data. This predictive capability allows the care team to proactively adjust the treatment plan or gather additional documentation before submission, minimizing delays and rework. It is also possible to incorporate feedback loops into the AI model, allowing it to continuously learn from denials and approvals to further refine its recommendations over time. This iterative learning process leads to higher accuracy, faster turnaround, and fewer appeals."

In addition to improving RCN, another clear economic benefit arises when leveraging GAI to reduce diagnostic errors and the associated costs of downstream complications. Diagnoses that are delayed or incorrect often lead to extended hospital stays, additional testing, and the potential for litigation or other financial liabilities. By accelerating and refining the diagnostic process, Gen AI helps ensure that patients receive the correct treatment earlier in their healthcare journey. This can minimize the cascading expenses that result from inaccurate or prolonged diagnostic odysseys. Even small improvements in diagnostic accuracy can generate substantial cost savings when aggregated across large patient populations, particularly in high-cost conditions such as cancer, chronic kidney disease, or heart failure.

Another financial advantage is the reduction of unnecessary or duplicative tests. In many hospital settings, a patient might undergo redundant imaging scans or laboratory tests, especially if they transfer between departments. Gen AI-based systems capable of consolidating patient data in real-time can alert clinicians that a particular test has already been performed or that an older image can be enhanced through generative algorithms rather than taking a new scan. This automation relieves the administrative and clinical burden of cross-referencing patient records while also cutting down on the direct costs of performing additional tests. The result is a more efficient flow of diagnostic activity that translates into budgetary relief for hospitals.

Moreover, Gen AI has the potential to reallocate valuable staff time. Tasks that are routinely viewed as time-sinks, such as sifting through extensive medical records or filling out patient discharge summaries, can be significantly accelerated or even automated by advanced language models. Freed from these administrative burdens, healthcare providers can devote more attention to direct patient care. This improved labor efficiency can reduce staffing costs over the long term or reorient staff toward value-adding activities. In a context where many healthcare systems face staffing shortages, reimagining the distribution of labor is not just a matter of cost savings but also a strategy for coping with systemic workforce challenges.

One must note, however, that realizing these economic benefits depends on the upfront costs of implementing Gen AI. Hospitals will need to invest in data infrastructure, training programs, and possibly new roles, such as the Chief AI Officer, who is dedicated to overseeing AI strategies. There is also the recurring expense of model maintenance and retraining, as well as potential upgrades to accommodate evolving regulations or newly discovered capabilities. Smaller clinics or resource-constrained settings might find these initial costs prohibitive unless they partner with technology vendors or rely on cloud-based solutions that lower hardware expenses. Yet, these costs can be viewed as a strategic investment with the potential for substantial returns. The key lies in adopting a thoughtful approach that ensures GAI technology is used where it can genuinely enhance patient care and operational efficiency. Overextension, or adopting AI for AI's sake, can result in resource misallocations that erode economic benefits.

As more hospitals and clinical networks adopt Gen AI, pooled data from these implementers will likely yield additional insights into cost savings. It could become easier, for example, to quantify how much a generative algorithm-based approach to triage reduces average hospital stay lengths. This quantitative feedback shared through peer-reviewed studies or collaborative forums will help refine and validate the economic case for Gen AI in healthcare. There is ample reason to believe that, given proper design and deployment, the technology will not merely recoup its implementation costs but also generate ongoing returns in the form of higher operational efficiency and better health outcomes.

Reducing Unnecessary Procedures and Hospital Admissions

One of the most significant drains on healthcare resources and a frequent source of frustration for patients stems from unnecessary procedures and hospital admissions. Studies over the years have documented how defensive medicine, fragmented care, and inadequate patient follow-up can contribute to procedures that confer minimal or no clinical benefit. Patients themselves often bear these burdens, whether in the form of financial costs, exposure to avoidable side effects, or the anxiety of undergoing invasive interventions. By introducing Gen AI into the care pathway, healthcare systems have begun to explore how advanced data analytics can pinpoint inefficiencies and reduce superfluous admissions, investigations, or treatments.

Preventing unnecessary procedures starts with a clearer grasp of patient risk profiles. A typical scenario might involve a physician ordering an expensive imaging study to rule out a rare condition, even when the patient's symptom profile strongly suggests a more common and benign cause. Through Gen AI, risk stratification models can leverage broad datasets to offer an evidence-based probability that a patient's presentation aligns with one diagnosis over another. The algorithm might analyze past medical history, lab values, or even unstructured notes in the patient's record, generating a "risk score" that clarifies the necessity—or lack thereof—of further invasive investigation. Rather than taking a conservative, all-encompassing approach that leads to tests with low yield, clinicians can be guided by a sophisticated measure of likelihood. This decreases the incidence of "just in case" procedures that impose costs without genuine benefits.

Similarly, Gen AI can be employed to identify patients at high risk for complications or readmissions. By recognizing warning signs that might otherwise be missed, these models can enable timely outpatient interventions, such as adjusting a medication regimen or scheduling a telemedicine consultation, thereby averting the need for an acute hospital stay. For instance, a patient with congestive heart failure might have changes in their daily weight or mild shifts in blood pressure that, when aggregated and analyzed by an AI system, signal an impending decompensation event. Alerting the care team early allows for a proactive response, perhaps administering diuretics or modifying dietary guidance, thus obviating a costly and distressing hospitalization. As these risk stratification tools mature, they could integrate seamlessly with patient wearables, home monitoring devices, and AI-driven virtual care platforms, fostering a more distributed model of care where hospitals intervene only when genuinely needed.

In parallel, generative models can propose alternative treatment pathways, some of which might be less invasive than traditional procedures. Rather than scheduling a patient for an expensive and potentially risky surgical intervention, an AI could suggest a proven course of conservative management based on an analysis of similar patients who achieved good outcomes through physical therapy, medication, or lifestyle changes. Such recommendations can encourage clinicians to adopt a watchful-waiting approach under certain conditions, provided that close monitoring is in place to respond rapidly if the patient's condition worsens. This approach resonates with the concept of "value-based care," a model that prioritizes treatments that have strong evidence of benefit relative to cost and risk.

Indeed, the cultural shift required to reduce unnecessary procedures is no small feat. Physicians might worry about malpractice concerns, particularly in litigious environments, and some patients might equate more tests and more aggressive interventions with better care. Here, Gen AI can serve as a decision-support ally, furnishing data-driven risk assessments that clinicians can communicate to patients. A conversation that once hinged on ambiguous reassurance can become a more informed discussion about probabilities, potential outcomes, and patient preferences. The availability of tangible metrics can help mitigate the psychological and legal pressures that lead to redundant procedures.

While these scenarios underscore Gen AI's potential to reduce unnecessary admissions and interventions, they also bring forth the continuing need for robust doctor-patient communication and shared decision-making. An AI-driven recommendation to forego a procedure should be contextualized by the clinician, who can explain why the new data supports a more conservative course of action. Patients, for their part, should be empowered to ask questions about the AI model's suggestion and how it pertains to their personal values and medical goals. When these elements converge—a reliable Gen AI system, competent clinicians, and informed patients- the healthcare system can operate with greater efficiency and a sharper focus on truly beneficial procedures.

Optimizing Resource Allocation in Healthcare Systems

Resource allocation and utilization are the hidden engine that underpins every aspect of healthcare delivery. While clinicians focus on diagnosing and treating patients, administrators wrestle with an equally formidable challenge: how to distribute funds, staff, equipment, and time in a manner that maximizes patient outcomes. Historically, these decisions have been guided by management principles, rudimentary data analytics, and political or institutional priorities. In more recent times, data-driven insights have improved administrators' abilities to forecast patient volumes, plan budgets, and manage supply chains. Gen AI adds another dimension to this process by enabling sophisticated simulations, predictive modeling, and dynamic reallocations that keep up with the ebb and flow of patient demand.

One way Gen AI optimizes resource allocation is by refining patient flow management. Emergency departments (EDs) often experience unpredictable surges in patient arrivals, resulting in extended wait times and suboptimal patient experiences. By analyzing historical data on admissions, weather patterns, local events, and even seasonal illness trends, Gen AI can predict potential spikes in ED visits or bed occupancy. This predictive capacity allows hospitals to reallocate staff, open additional triage areas, or postpone non-urgent procedures in anticipation of a surge. It also informs advanced scheduling for operating rooms, ensuring that emergency surgeries do not clash with elective procedures and reducing unnecessary cancellations or delays. Over time, these subtle but continuous adjustments can yield significant improvements in how effectively a hospital uses its existing facilities and workforce.

Inventory Management and Asset Utilization

Inventory management offers another domain where Gen AI can add value. Hospitals maintain large inventories of medications, surgical supplies, and medical devices. Over-ordering leads to wasted expenditure, while under-ordering threatens patient care by creating shortages. Traditional inventory systems typically rely on threshold-based reordering, which may not account for patient acuity changes or shifting treatment protocols. Gen AI models, on the other hand, can track real-time usage rates, analyze correlations between patient diagnoses and medication requirements, and forecast future demands based on upcoming scheduled procedures. Armed with these insights, administrators can make informed decisions about how much stock to keep on hand, reducing both wastage and the risk of shortages.

A particularly high-stakes arena for resource optimization is the utilization of expensive medical imaging devices—MRI machines, CT scanners, and other advanced diagnostic tools. The cost of these machines is substantial, and every hour they remain idle can translate into significant financial losses for the institution. At the same time, patient wait times for scans can balloon if scheduling is poorly managed, leading to diagnostic delays that can negatively affect clinical outcomes and patient satisfaction.

Gen AI can help balance this equation by analyzing scheduling data, patient flow, and case urgency to create a dynamic allocation plan for high-value equipment. Rather than relying on a static timetable or manually coordinated scheduling blocks, an AI model could continuously monitor multiple data points: incoming patient referrals, staff shift changes, machine maintenance schedules, and even projected wait times for key departments. With this real-time intelligence, the AI can slot patients in more efficiently, ensuring minimal downtime between scans and reducing the likelihood of machines sitting idle.

If, for instance, the model notices an unexpected dip in scheduled scans around midday, it might automatically prompt the radiology department to move outpatient appointments forward from the afternoon, thus preventing the machine from going unutilized. Conversely, if an uptick in ED patients is predicted for the late afternoon, the AI can reserve enough scanner capacity to accommodate urgent cases. Such flexible scheduling is particularly valuable for large hospitals that see not only routine imaging but also urgent and emergent cases arriving unpredictably throughout the day.

Moreover, the data gathered by Gen AI systems can highlight trends over time, revealing bottlenecks in imaging workflows. For example, the model might discover that a particular machine is frequently underutilized on weekends due to staffing limitations or that a certain hour of the day sees repeated scheduling conflicts with the operating room's imaging needs. Administrators and radiology directors can then take informed steps to adjust staffing, stagger machine usage, or adjust appointment lengths to meet actual patient demand. Over the long term, this data-driven approach helps leadership make strategic decisions about whether to invest in more scanners, reallocate existing ones, or optimize maintenance schedules to align with periods of low patient volume.

Human Resource Management

Human resource management is similarly enhanced when Gen AI is leveraged for more precise staffing strategies. In many settings, shift assignments remain relatively static, determined by historical norms or top-level directives. However, patient demand fluctuates considerably, influenced by factors as varied as local demographic changes, climate conditions, or viral outbreaks. By recognizing these patterns, Gen AI can suggest where additional staffing is most needed or whether it is feasible to offer remote services in certain cases. In rural areas, for instance, telemedicine consultations might alleviate the burden on a limited number of specialty providers, enabling them to focus on high-acuity cases in person while lower-acuity cases are handled virtually. This alignment of staffing with actual demand not only improves patient access to care but also boosts morale by preventing staff from being overextended.

Public Health and Broader Allocation Implications

The potential for Gen AI to optimize resource allocation extends to macro-level considerations as well. Public health authorities, for instance, could incorporate generative models into their planning for pandemics or large-scale public health crises. By simulating the spread of an infectious disease under different policy scenarios, such as school closures or vaccination campaigns, they can better predict hospital capacity requirements, the need for additional quarantine facilities, or the timing of partial lockdowns. Such strategic forecasting is not purely reactive; it allows for preemptive planning that can save both lives and economic resources.

Still, the effectiveness of Gen AI for resource allocation hinges on data quality, interoperability, and governance. If the underlying EHR or hospital management systems are out-of-date or siloed, the AI's insights may be incomplete. Moreover, shifting organizational cultures can pose an obstacle, as administrators and department heads may resist ceding any control to algorithmic suggestions, even when those suggestions come with strong data support. Hence, the integration process typically requires pilot programs, transparent performance metrics, and steady communication about the AI's rationale. As these tools gain acceptance and trust, they begin to operate more seamlessly in real-time, offering micro-adjustments that collectively yield large-scale improvements.

At a philosophical level, resource allocation in healthcare is about balancing the moral imperative of patient care with the practical constraints of budgets and logistical capacities. Gen AI does not replace that moral calculus, nor does it absolve decision-makers of ethical responsibility. Instead, it furnishes them with a more detailed map of what is possible and probable in various scenarios. Those who use these tools effectively can uncover creative ways to distribute limited resources so that they do the greatest good for the greatest number of patients. This synergy between moral reasoning and sophisticated analytics stands as one of Gen AI's most meaningful contributions to the evolving landscape of healthcare delivery.

The Current and Future Impact of AI Agents

As Gen AI continues to reshape clinical routines and medical research, an emerging frontier known as AI agents is poised to revolutionize healthcare delivery even further. AI agents, in simple terms, move beyond narrow tasks—like identifying anomalies on a chest X-ray or predicting medication dosages—and act as orchestrators capable of handling multiple objectives across diverse domains. They can integrate specialized AI modules, communicate with EHR systems, analyze patient data in real-time, and even engage in patient interactions via chat interfaces or other mediums.

In many industries, these AI agents already enhance customer experience by offering personalized support and guidance. For instance, banking customers often consult automated agents that manage account queries and provide financial advice. In retail, AI-driven assistants predict consumer preferences and assist with shopping recommendations. Transport and logistics firms use intelligent agents to optimize delivery routes, track inventories, and engage with customers about shipping schedules. Through such applications, AI agents deliver real-time assistance that is adaptive, context-aware, and capable of learning from user feedback.

In healthcare, this multitasking potential of AI agents is already manifesting in varied ways. Some hospitals deploy agents to streamline patient triage by evaluating symptoms, medical histories, and demographic data all at once and then directing patients to the correct department. Other agents facilitate patient communications, whether it is scheduling follow-up appointments, providing medication reminders, or clarifying discharge instructions. By bridging multiple data streams and interfacing with both clinicians and patients, AI agents reduce administrative burdens and decrease the risk of fragmented care. Their capacity to engage patients around the clock—often in multiple languages or with support for individuals with disabilities—expands accessibility and can greatly enhance the overall patient experience.

Looking forward, AI agents have the potential to orchestrate entire care pathways, coordinating specialists, managing resource allocations, and monitoring patient progress. Imagine an autonomous "care conductor" that continuously evaluates bed availability, staffing constraints, and patient needs, making real-time adjustments to balance the load and prioritize critical cases. For chronic disease management, an AI agent could proactively track a patient's biometric data, recommend lifestyle modifications when early warning signs appear, and schedule telehealth consultations if needed. Such a system would free healthcare professionals to focus on higher-level decision-making and more nuanced patient interactions while still maintaining a robust safety net that flags outliers or emergencies.

Yet, as with all AI innovations, the rollout of AI agents in healthcare must be guided by transparent governance, stringent quality checks, and thoughtful user experience design. Concerns about data privacy, unintended biases, and overdependence on automated decision-making grow more pronounced as AI agents expand their scope. Ensuring that clinicians remain in the loop and that patients understand the nature of AI-driven assistance is paramount to preserving trust. Still, the foundational promise is monumental: real-time, context-sensitive assistance can not only streamline healthcare delivery but also help usher in a new era of GAI-centric medicine, where autonomous systems and human experts partner more seamlessly than ever before.

Concluding Reflections on Gen AI's Transformative Role

As we examine Gen AI's impact on healthcare delivery, a pattern emerges: the technology serves as both a mirror and a magnifier for challenges and opportunities that have long existed in medicine. It reflects the intricacy of diagnosing diseases, planning treatments, and managing healthcare systems by revealing hidden correlations and emergent risks. At the same time, it magnifies the potential for more precise, cost-effective, and patient-centric care by unlocking forms of analysis that simply were not feasible in earlier eras. From assisting in the early detection of cancer to crafting highly individualized treatment plans,

Gen AI spans the spectrum of patient care, steering it toward a future that is less reactive and more proactive.

This transformation does not unfold in a vacuum. It intersects with regulatory policies that seek to ensure the safety and efficacy of AI applications. It intersects with organizational cultures that may be more or less open to technological disruption. It intersects with economic realities that force health systems to consider value propositions and return on investment. And it intersects, most importantly, with the trust patients place in their care providers, a trust that can either be bolstered by the transparent use of AI or eroded by opaque algorithms that diminish human interaction.

Perhaps the most profound aspect of Gen AI's impact is its catalytic effect on changing the mindset of healthcare professionals by shifting focus from "sick care" to preventive care and the early initiation of treatments. By enabling personalized strategies that adapt to each individual's unique biology and circumstances, it underscores the reality that no two patients are identical. By highlighting the economic gains possible through reduced wastage and more rational resource allocation, it advocates for the idea that quality healthcare and cost-effectiveness need not be at odds. Rather, when AI is woven thoughtfully into clinical practice, both patients and institutions stand to benefit.

Where does this leave us in the broader journey of healthcare innovation? The chapters so far have charted a path from the conceptual underpinnings of Gen AI to the finer points of its implementation. We have explored challenges—ethical, regulatory, and organizational—and traced how they influence adoption timelines. We have also looked to real-world examples of AI-driven progress, from pioneering startups to major hospital systems that have piloted or deployed Gen AI tools with encouraging results. Amid these stories and data points, one fact resonates consistently: Gen AI does not diminish the role of the human clinician. Rather, it redefines that role, freeing medical experts from certain menial tasks, expanding the scope of information they can process, and ultimately helping them deliver care that is more consistent, equitable, and precise.

Yet even the most enthusiastic supporters of Gen AI would concede that the technology remains a work in progress. Future directions might see an even deeper integration of wearable biosensors, advanced robotics for assisted surgeries, or expanded telemedicine platforms that rely on generative models for triage in remote regions. Over time, we may witness the evolution of Gen AI from a specialized tool into a ubiquitous presence in every aspect of healthcare, from routine check-ups to advanced life-saving interventions. In that world, the emphasis will be on continuous learning, both for the AI systems, which must stay updated with the latest clinical evidence, and for the practitioners, who must remain vigilant about the boundaries and biases of algorithmic decision-making.

It is this dynamic interplay between technological capability and human judgment, between economic imperatives and patient welfare, between incremental improvements and visionary leaps—that defines the transformative power of Gen AI in healthcare. As we proceed to the next chapters, we will delve even deeper into the metrics by which Gen AI's success can be measured, the organizational strategies that maximize its potential, and the ethical frameworks that must evolve in tandem. For now, suffice it to say that Gen AI's role in healthcare delivery is no longer a matter of speculation. It is an ever-expanding reality, one that promises a future where patients are diagnosed earlier, treated more effectively, and guided through a healthcare experience that is both compassionate and deeply data-driven.

Chapter 9

GAI in Medical Research and Drug Discovery

AI tools, including generative models, are giving us new ways to interpret medical data and develop hypotheses that would take humans years to uncover. This technology is not just assisting, but transforming the nature of how medical research is conducted.

Peter Lee, Corporate Vice President of Research and Incubation at Microsoft

Generative artificial intelligence (GAI) has emerged as a dynamic force in healthcare, reshaping clinical workflows, diagnoses, and patient management in ways that were scarcely imaginable a decade ago. Yet, while these applications may be the most visible face of AI in medicine, GAI's impact on drug discovery and broader medical research is every bit as profound. The process of bringing a new therapeutic agent to market is typically long, risky, and enormously expensive. Researchers must identify viable drug targets, sift through countless compounds, validate the safety and efficacy of lead candidates, and navigate multiple phases of clinical trials. Even with the support of traditional computational methods, the timeline for developing a novel drug often spans a decade or more, accompanied by a staggering financial burden; because of this, very few drugs make it to the market, and those that do have gone through a very lengthy and expensive process. Even once they are approved, the patent may only extend for ten years. That might sound like a lot of time, but compared to the amount of money that may have been invested in the approval process, it is a limited window to recoup that investment. It can take

DOI: 10.4324/9781003665434-9

a decade or more to bring a drug to market, and it can cost billions with a "b." Furthermore, that is the cost of "success." It does not even take into account the losses incurred by drugs that fail and do not even make it through the approval process.

Into this arduous landscape steps GAI, offering new levels of efficiency in molecule generation, target validation, and patient selection for clinical trials. As technology advances, GAI appears poised to integrate seamlessly with the best practices of pharmaceutical science, potentially ushering in an era where drug discovery is not merely sped up but also fundamentally transformed.

Traditional AI, ML, and Their Transformative Effect on Drug Discovery

As discussed in great length in my first book, *Quantum Care: A Deep Dive into AI for Health Delivery and Research, f*or decades, computational approaches to drug discovery have revolved around speeding up processes that would otherwise rely on laborious benchwork and trial-and-error experimentation. At the outset, researchers focused on relatively simple algorithms for quantitative structure-activity relationships (QSAR), which correlated certain molecular features with biological activity. These algorithms evolved into more sophisticated ML methods as computing power grew and data sets expanded. By harnessing the wealth of chemical, genomic, and proteomic data produced over years of scientific investigation, these methods began to identify potential drug targets and lead compounds faster than purely manual methods could achieve.

Predictive modeling has been at the heart of these transformations. Organizations like Atomwise used deep learning to predict molecular binding affinities, assisting researchers in selecting promising compounds for further development. Virtual screening became another key tool, allowing pharmaceutical companies to rapidly evaluate vast libraries of molecules for potential efficacy against a target protein, thus eliminating large swaths of compounds before moving to the more expensive phases of physical testing. Virtual screening is often coupled with high-throughput techniques that experimentally confirm whether a modeled interaction holds true under laboratory conditions. This synergy between computational and empirical screening has already shaved months or even years off the drug discovery timeline in certain cases.

Beyond screening, the industry has seen the rise of in silico research, which uses computer-based simulations to explore drug behavior under different physiological conditions. Digital twinning—an approach initially popularized in engineering and manufacturing—has found its way into healthcare, where researchers construct digital replicas of biological systems, organs, or entire patient profiles. By introducing a new drug compound into this virtual environment, researchers can observe predicted responses, side-effect profiles, and potential toxicities long before any patient is administered the drug. Such digital twins also allow for modifications in dosage, drug combinations, or route of administration to see how these adjustments might influence efficacy and safety. This iterative cycle of modeling, virtual testing, and refining replaces a portion of the guesswork inherent in traditional lab-based methods, reducing the need for extensive wet-lab experiments.

A notable real-world example that encapsulates these advancements is the work done by companies like Schrödinger, whose computational platforms have been used by pharmaceutical giants to optimize lead candidates for specific targets. Another example is BenevolentAI, which applies machine learning to build knowledge graphs that highlight novel links between diseases, genes, and compounds. While these ventures are still associated more with conventional AI and ML rather than fully generative approaches, they have paved the way for the next generation of drug discovery technologies. The results are encouraging, resulting in faster identification of viable leads, lower development costs, and more robust scientific rationales for the path from target selection to clinical trials.

Yet even these successes highlight certain constraints. Predictive models are often limited to the chemical space that researchers are already aware of or to known interactions and curated libraries. Virtual screening can drastically narrow the field, but does not necessarily invent new chemical entities from scratch. While digital twins and in silico experiments offer crucial insights, they still rely heavily on the quality and breadth of the input data. These constraints are precisely where GAI brings a fresh wave of innovation, offering the capacity to generate novel hypotheses, synthesize entirely new molecular structures, and, perhaps most intriguingly, adapt to new data in an iterative, creative manner reminiscent of a human researcher's scientific intuition.

How GAI Is Accelerating Drug Discovery and Development Processes

A distinctive hallmark of generative models is their ability to produce new content, whether in the form of text, images, or—in the context of pharmaceutical research—molecular structures. Unlike discriminative models, which classify or predict based on existing data, generative models can be trained to learn the underlying principles of chemical space, protein folding, or drug-target interactions. Once these principles are grasped, the AI can systematically "invent" compounds that fit certain parameters, such as binding affinity or ADME (absorption, distribution, metabolism, and excretion) properties. This shift from classification to creation heralds an era in which the search for drug candidates is not confined to known chemical libraries but can extend into potentially infinite chemical territory.

In practical terms, generative models can be employed at multiple points along the drug discovery pipeline. Early in the discovery process, they can produce thousands of candidate molecules that exhibit a high theoretical probability of binding to the target. These candidates can then be refined via iterative feedback loops, where the model "learns" from experimental data on synthesized compounds. When a handful of promising leads fail toxicity tests, for example, the algorithm updates its internal parameters to avoid repeating those molecular features. This cyclical approach—often referred to as closed-loop drug discovery—reduces the time wasted on repeated synthetic dead ends and offers a level of flexibility that surpasses the more rigid screening processes of earlier AI generations.

GAI can also play a critical role in designing more potent and selective molecules for complex targets like protein-protein interfaces, which have historically been considered challenging or "undruggable." Through advanced modeling of three-dimensional protein structures, generative algorithms can infer how small changes in a molecule's conformation or side chain might enhance binding specificity. In some cases, GAI even contemplates alternative scaffolds or ring systems that human chemists might never have considered, broadening the horizon of potential drug candidates.

Drug repurposing, another strategy that has gained momentum, also benefits from GAI. Traditional repurposing efforts have scoured existing libraries of FDA-approved or clinically tested compounds to see if they might be effective for other indications. GAI can offer more creative matches by suggesting modifications to known compounds that preserve beneficial properties while adjusting for new targets. This approach was spotlighted during the COVID-19 pandemic, as multiple organizations raced to either adapt existing antiviral drugs or design new ones. Generative models provided a systematic way to propose variations of known molecules, accelerating the screening and testing processes.

Companies such as Insilico Medicine and Exscientia exemplify the impact of generative approaches. Insilico Medicine has showcased an AI-generated compound that successfully advanced through preclinical testing in record time, while Exscientia claims to have a pipeline of AI-designed molecules that address a variety of diseases. Though these firms are still subject to the stringent validations required by regulators, their progress signals that GAI-driven pipelines are feasible and can, under the right conditions, expedite early stage drug development. The real challenge is translating these lab-based and computational triumphs into sustainable improvements in cost-effectiveness and success rates across the entire industry.

Regulatory scrutiny remains a factor. A drug candidate designed by an AI must still demonstrate safety and efficacy through clinical trials, and the novelty of GAI can prompt questions about how best to validate the digital aspects of design. However, regulatory agencies have already shown a willingness to adapt, providing evolving guidelines for AI-driven drug development, including frameworks for verifying the reliability of generative models. In parallel, pharmaceutical companies are developing internal governance structures to ensure that the creative output of GAI aligns with evidence-based scientific rigor. The result is a growing sense of optimism that GAI can integrate seamlessly with the current regime of translational science, bridging the gap between computational hypotheses and real-world therapeutics.

Accelerated Clinical Trials through GAI-Driven Patient Selection

The drug discovery pipeline does not end once a promising compound is identified. Clinical trials, especially in later phases, are often the most protracted and costly part of drug development. Recruiting suitable patients, managing trial sites, maintaining compliance, and collecting clinically relevant data can take years. GAI offers a powerful mechanism for accelerating these processes, primarily by improving how patients are selected, stratified, and monitored throughout the trial.

A common hurdle in clinical research is enrollment that either fails to meet targets or enrolls patients who do not reflect the real-world population. In some cases, a lack of diversity in trial participants can lead to skewed efficacy and safety profiles, causing problems when the drug hits the market. GAI-powered models can sift through enormous patient databases, including EHRs, genetic information, and even social determinants of health, to identify those who are most likely to benefit from or respond to the investigational drug. By narrowing the pool early on, pharmaceutical sponsors and clinical research organizations (CROs) can reduce the number of participants needed for a given study, or they can ensure that the trial includes a demographically balanced cohort. This approach lowers the probability of having to repeat phases or adjust protocols due to incomplete or suboptimal enrollment.

Once the trial is underway, GAI can be used to track patient data in real-time, potentially flagging signs that a participant is responding differently than expected. This capacity for dynamic patient stratification allows researchers to adapt their protocols. They might, for instance, transfer a patient to a different treatment arm if early biomarkers suggest they are more aligned with another subset. While such adaptive trial designs have existed for some time, GAI takes them to a new level by forecasting how certain genetic or phenotypic markers correlate with success or adverse events. In doing so, the technology moves beyond static, one-size-fits-all trial structures and into a more fluid, evidence-driven model of clinical investigation.

An added benefit is the ability to identify potential safety signals earlier. Algorithms that continuously scan patient data can detect patterns that might presage a serious side effect. By spotting these signals early, researchers can modify dosages or halt a trial arm altogether, mitigating risk to participants. This not only accelerates the path to understanding a drug's true safety profile but also reassures regulators that any emerging problems will be swiftly and proactively addressed. Several large pharmaceutical companies, including Pfizer and Roche, have experimented with AI-driven patient recruitment and monitoring strategies. While not all of these initiatives explicitly involve generative models, the next wave of tools promises to incorporate generative capabilities that can simulate a range of patient outcomes, thus refining trial protocols on the fly.

These enhancements to the clinical trial process tie back to the overarching theme of GAI's potential in drug development: harnessing the power of comprehensive data insights, real-time analytics, and creative modeling to reduce wasted resources and keep trials targeted on patient populations where the drug is most likely to succeed. By making every step—from enrollment to monitoring—more efficient and data-driven, GAI can alleviate bottlenecks that have long plagued traditional research methods. If early stage drug discovery exemplifies GAI's creative force, then advanced clinical trials illustrate how that creativity can be harnessed to produce a safer, faster, and more patient-centric process.

Facilitating Precision Medicine and Personalized Treatment Approaches

As medicine moves ever closer to a future of individualized care, GAI stands poised to become one of its primary enablers. Conventional drug discovery has often aimed at broad populations, generating blockbuster drugs that help many but may also leave certain subpopulations underserved or facing disproportionate side effects. The emerging paradigm of precision medicine shifts the focus from one-size-fits-all solutions to targeted interventions based on a patient's genetic, molecular, and clinical profile. GAI enhances this transition by managing the sheer complexity of data required to personalize treatments effectively.

One obvious intersection between GAI and precision medicine lies in the analysis of genomic and proteomic data. With next-generation sequencing (NGS) now widely available, researchers grapple with massive datasets on patient genetics, tumor markers, and disease signatures. Sifting through this ocean of information to identify which genetic mutations are truly driving disease—and which might be red herrings—demands advanced computational strategies. GAI can do more than simply label or rank variants; it can hypothesize molecular mechanisms that link certain mutations to disease pathways. This capability extends to synthesizing new compounds specifically tailored to shut down or modulate those pathways, bridging the gap between discovering a genetic anomaly and developing a therapeutic molecule that precisely targets it.

In oncology, for instance, patients with the same clinical diagnosis can have tumors that are strikingly different at the molecular level. A therapy that works for one patient might be completely ineffective for another. GAI-assisted precision medicine uses large-scale molecular and clinical data to stratify these patients into subpopulations, each with a unique genetic or proteomic signature, and then designs targeted treatments, either from existing drug libraries or newly generated molecules. By systematically iterating on molecular structures, GAI can produce variations optimized for each subpopulation's molecular configuration, effectively customizing therapies at a fine-grained level.

Another dimension of personalized therapy involves a more dynamic approach to patient management. If the disease evolves or if resistance to a particular drug emerges, GAI can generate new treatment candidates or propose combination therapies that thwart resistance mechanisms. This adaptive, iterative cycle—treat, observe, revise—has the potential to transform chronic diseases like rheumatoid arthritis, certain cancers, or neurological disorders into manageable conditions rather than progressive ailments. The data gleaned from each patient's response can feed back into generative models, making them even more adept at anticipating how a disease might mutate or resist. Over time, this feedback loop could create an environment in which personalized medicine is not just a lofty vision but a daily reality for clinicians and patients.

Companies at the forefront of precision medicine are increasingly integrating GAI into their workflows. Tempus, for example, aggregates and analyzes massive amounts of patient molecular data to help oncologists devise targeted treatment plans. While their platform relies on multiple AI strategies, the addition of generative modeling could make the service more agile, generating personalized drug combinations or dosage schedules tailored to a patient's unique genetic signature. Similarly, platforms that manage large-scale genomic data, like Illumina's BaseSpace, could harness generative models to map out potential therapeutic interventions in real time, bridging the gap between genotype and clinical action.

These developments also carry ethical and regulatory considerations. Personalized therapies sometimes challenge the conventional notion of population-level risk assessment, demanding new frameworks for evaluating efficacy and safety. If GAI suggests a unique compound for a small cohort of patients, how can regulators ensure that the therapy undergoes sufficient testing? Large-scale, randomized trials may not be practical for very specific genetic subtypes. In response, regulatory bodies and research institutions are exploring adaptive trial designs and real-world evidence (RWE) models that gather robust data on small but genetically distinct populations. The result could be an entirely new tapestry of clinical research, woven more from individualized threads than from broad-stroke guidelines.

Tailoring Treatments Based on Genetic and Molecular Data

GAI's role in tailoring treatments does not end with broad categories of disease or general patient subpopulations. Within precision medicine, the finer challenge is bridging the final gap between macro-level genetic insights and the micro-level molecular mechanisms that underlie pathology. This demands the capacity to analyze data from a variety of sources—genomic sequencing, proteomics, metabolomics, and epigenetics—and to synthesize actionable knowledge that clinicians can use. It also requires the creative spark that generative models offer, the ability to propose new hypotheses or molecular agents that might not follow conventional chemical logic.

One promising avenue is the targeted design of small molecules or biologics that latch onto unique protein isoforms expressed in certain patient subtypes. GAI can parse massive databases of protein structures, identify distinctive binding pockets, and engineer molecules that fit those pockets with high specificity. Whereas traditional drug design might use computational docking programs limited to known chemical entities, GAI can conjure new scaffolds if it recognizes that an unconventional arrangement of atoms could improve specificity or reduce off-target effects. This imaginative leap has the potential to eliminate a major cause of adverse events in drug therapy: binding to the "wrong" target or inadvertently influencing vital biological pathways.

In oncology, many research teams employ GAI to tackle the complexity of tumor heterogeneity. A single tumor might harbor multiple clones, each with different mutations and growth dynamics. By analyzing real-time genomic data from biopsy samples, GAI can theoretically propose multi-agent regimens that take into account the diversity within the tumor mass. If one subpopulation of tumor cells has developed a mutation conferring resistance to Drug A, but remains vulnerable to Drug B, the generative model can fine-tune the ratio of these agents or propose a third compound to address emergent forms of resistance. This approach transforms cancer care from a linear progression of monotherapies to a dynamic, data-driven balancing act, optimizing outcomes at each stage of the disease.

Beyond cancer, diseases such as cystic fibrosis, Alzheimer's, or certain rare genetic disorders stand to benefit from GAI's capacity to design targeted therapies. When a disease results from a specific genetic mutation that alters a single protein's function, the therapeutic challenge is typically to correct or compensate for that singular defect. GAI can screen or design molecules that restore the protein's native conformation, improve its trafficking, or modulate downstream pathways affected by the mutation. This might be especially beneficial for rare diseases where the patient population is too small to attract large-scale research investment using traditional methods. GAI's efficiency can lower the economic threshold for exploring niche conditions, potentially leading to breakthroughs for underserved groups.

Nevertheless, the integration of GAI for molecular-level customization requires robust infrastructure for data sharing and privacy. Genetic data is highly sensitive and must be managed within secure environments that comply with regulations such as HIPAA or GDPR. The diverse data types—ranging from imaging to molecular profiling—also challenge the interoperability of existing hospital and research data systems. Institutions that succeed in harnessing GAI for personalized therapy typically have well-established data pipelines, cross-functional teams, and strong collaborations with biotech or pharmaceutical companies. Under those conditions, the synergy between genetic insights and generative modeling may allow clinicians to move beyond broad disease labels, forging an era of truly bespoke treatments anchored in molecular and genetic precision.

Identifying Patient Subpopulations for Targeted Therapies

While GAI's creative potential is most evident in the generation of novel molecules, it also excels at one of the most fundamental tasks in medicine: classification. Generative models can be trained on clinical, molecular, and imaging datasets to generate patient "profiles" that cluster individuals into subpopulations with shared features. Unlike conventional clustering algorithms, which simply partition data, generative models can elaborate on why certain clusters form and even simulate hypothetical patients belonging to each group. These capabilities offer a robust way to discover or validate subpopulations that respond differently to the same therapy.

This approach can be seen in practice when pharmaceutical companies integrate RWE from electronic health records or registries into their GAI-driven pipelines. For instance, a drug that shows moderate efficacy across a broad population may actually be highly effective for a smaller subset characterized by a specific genotype or biomarker pattern. Identifying that subset can be the key to successful Phase III trials or post-market strategies. By isolating and focusing on this group, researchers can design more targeted studies, thereby increasing the likelihood of demonstrating a strong therapeutic effect. In the past, such subgroup identification might have been a post hoc exercise, revealing itself only when analyzing trial data after the fact. With GAI-based analysis, subpopulations can emerge much earlier, allowing for refined inclusion criteria from the outset of the clinical program.

Subpopulation discovery is also relevant in the context of combination therapies. A generative model might detect that a patient group with a certain pattern of immune markers responds better to immunotherapy combined with a targeted agent rather than either treatment alone. By simulating various dosage schedules and synergy effects, GAI can hypothesize which subpopulation is most likely to benefit from the combination. Clinical trials can then test these hypotheses directly, potentially saving time and expense compared to a broad approach that lumps all patients together and dilutes the therapeutic signal.

Some institutions have deployed GAI for subpopulation identification in metabolic disorders such as Type 2 diabetes, a condition that can manifest with widely varying degrees of insulin resistance, obesity-related factors, and cardiovascular complications. If GAI pinpoints a particular subset of patients who are prone to rapid disease progression under certain dietary habits, clinicians can intervene more aggressively or even personalize medication regimens to address those specific risk factors. The overarching objective is to prevent complications, avoid hospitalizations, and reduce the need for more costly interventions down the line. By tailoring therapies to these precisely defined groups, the healthcare system moves closer to an ideal scenario in which each patient receives a treatment strategy grounded in the specifics of their clinical and molecular profile.

Still, a cautionary note is in order. While subpopulation analysis can elevate precision medicine, it also risks fragmenting patient groups so narrowly that clinical trials lose statistical power. Researchers must balance the desire for customized care with the practical requirements of establishing efficacy in a sufficiently large sample. Moreover, rare subpopulations might face challenges in recruitment. Here, GAI can again lend support by predicting how smaller groups might respond, thus enabling more flexible, adaptive trial designs. The aim is not just to produce subpopulation insights but to integrate them cohesively with the larger drug development framework, ensuring that each finding is actionable and scientifically robust.

Success Stories in Drug Discovery Facilitated by GAI

Although the application of GAI to drug discovery is still relatively new, several success stories illustrate the tangible benefits of generative models in real-world pharmaceutical contexts. One often-cited example is the rapid discovery of a candidate molecule by Insilico Medicine designed to target a particular fibrosis pathway. Insilico claimed to have used a generative model to propose an entirely novel scaffold, which was subsequently verified through preclinical experiments. By closing the feedback loop between synthetic data generation, AI-driven hypothesis testing, and wet-lab validation, the company condensed a process that might typically take years into a matter of months. While clinical trial outcomes for such molecules will provide the ultimate verdict, the speed and efficiency of reaching this juncture are noteworthy.

Exscientia, a UK-based firm, has also gained attention for its AI-driven pipeline. The company has multiple collaborations with major pharmaceutical players like Sanofi and Bayer, aiming to leverage generative models for targeted oncology and immunology compounds. In one publicized case, Exscientia advanced an AI-designed drug candidate for obsessive-compulsive disorder (OCD) into Phase I clinical trials in less than a year from project inception—a remarkable milestone compared to traditional development timelines. That candidate's trajectory, pending clinical outcomes, offers a glimpse of how GAI can operate in tandem with rigorous scientific processes.

Yet another success story underscores GAI's role in optimizing existing compounds. Recursion Pharmaceuticals has been using AI to generate new insights into cellular phenotypes, repurposing known molecules for additional indications. While not exclusively dedicated to GAI, Recursion employs advanced computational techniques that border on generative approaches, illuminating novel therapeutic opportunities that might otherwise remain hidden. Each success not only garners attention but also propels the field forward, prompting regulators to adapt frameworks and inspiring researchers to push the boundaries of generative design.

The utility of GAI is by no means confined to small molecules. Protein engineering—a domain revolutionized by the advent of DeepMind's AlphaFold, albeit not strictly generative in the sense of novel design—has also seen generative approaches that propose new protein structures with particular binding properties or enzymatic functions. These proteins could serve as biological drugs or as catalysts in synthetic pathways, opening possibilities that reach far beyond conventional pharmaceuticals. Startups focused on protein design, such as Generate Biomedicines, harness generative models to craft entirely new proteins aimed at specific therapeutic tasks, from binding to a viral spike protein to modulating an immune receptor. While still emerging, these efforts suggest that GAI's creative prowess can extend to complex biomolecules, broadening the scope of drug discovery well into the biological frontiers.

Yet another emblematic story, especially relevant in light of the global COVID-19 pandemic, involves the use of AI at Moderna—one of the primary biotech companies involved in Operation Warp Speed, the U.S. government's program to accelerate vaccine development. While the mRNA platform itself offers inherent speed in generating vaccine candidates, researchers can synthesize mRNA sequences rapidly once they know a pathogen's genetic code. Moderna also harnessed advanced computational tools, including AI-driven analytics, to refine the design and testing of their vaccine candidates. Because mRNA vaccines hinge on selecting precise genetic constructs that encode immunogenic viral proteins, AI and machine learning models helped Moderna more efficiently identify which mRNA sequences were most likely to produce robust, targeted immune responses.

During Operation Warp Speed, this synergy of mRNA technology and AI-driven design shaved precious time off traditional vaccine development. Instead of expending months or years on empirical trial-and-error, researchers leveraged computational predictions to narrow the field to a handful of highly promising candidates for further preclinical and clinical evaluation. While the ultimate speed of vaccine availability also depended on massive funding, regulatory agility, and simultaneous clinical trials, AI was part of the engine that enabled Moderna to respond so quickly once the novel coronavirus genome was published. The near-historic pace at which the COVID-19 vaccines were authorized—less than a year from initial design to emergency use—underscored how advanced computational models, generative approaches, and data-driven validation can accelerate the trajectory of drug (and vaccine) development under urgent circumstances.

These examples—Insilico Medicine's fibrosis compound, Exscientia's swift candidate for OCD, and Moderna's AI-assisted COVID-19 vaccine development—collectively highlight the promise of GAI and AI-driven innovation. They illustrate that speed and invention need not come at the expense of scientific rigor. Each success also underscores the importance of integrating computational ingenuity with rigorous clinical validation and agile regulatory pathways.

As GAI continues to evolve, the pharmaceutical industry stands at the threshold of a new paradigm in which drug discovery can respond with heightened speed and precision to both global crises and everyday healthcare needs.

Reflections on the Future of GAI in Drug Discovery

The shift from traditional computational methods to GAI signals more than just incremental improvement; it suggests a fundamental change in how researchers conceive of drug discovery. Where older AI techniques often relied on classification or regression tasks to filter pre-existing libraries, GAI steps into the role of a creative collaborator capable of proposing genuinely novel solutions. Coupled with the capacity for real-time adaptation, the technology can reinvent the discovery pipeline, especially when woven seamlessly into translational research that moves from bench to bedside.

Clinical trials, another bottleneck in traditional drug development, are ripe for disruption through GAI-driven patient stratification and dynamic monitoring. The potential to reduce trial durations and costs while improving patient safety has attracted both industry giants and nimble startups. As data infrastructures become more robust and regulatory bodies continue updating their frameworks for AI-empowered trials, we may see a generation of therapeutics whose clinical validation is not only more efficient but also more ethically transparent, thanks to algorithms designed to identify adverse events early.

This same synergy reverberates in the realm of precision medicine. By fusing genomic data and real-world patient outcomes, GAI can enable the kind of hyper-personalized interventions that have long been a dream in medicine. The challenge is translating the output of generative models into clinical practice, forging links with physicians, payers, and, most crucially, patients themselves. Nonetheless, the successes in generating new compounds, optimizing dosage regimens, and identifying subpopulations foreshadow a future where the boundary between "bench science" and "bedside care" becomes increasingly permeable, with GAI bridging the gap.

Of course, the paradigm shift is not without its risks. The continued reliance on large, high-quality datasets raises concerns about data access, privacy, and the potential for bias that excludes underrepresented populations. Researchers must remain vigilant that GAI does not accelerate the development of compounds only relevant to wealthy markets, thereby deepening health disparities. Moreover, the question of interpretability remains central: even if GAI can design a potent molecule, clinicians and regulators alike will demand clear explanations of how it functions and why it is deemed safe.

Balancing these ethical and practical concerns is integral to ensure that the pharmaceutical field does not simply chase the newest AI trend but rather adopts generative tools as part of a deliberate, responsible strategy. Institutions that integrate GAI responsibly stand to reap enormous benefits: shorter timelines, reduced costs, fewer failures, and more individualized therapeutics that resonate with the diversity of patient needs. These outcomes, in turn, reinforce the promise that GAI holds for revolutionizing healthcare beyond the walls of drug discovery, potentially touching every aspect of preventive medicine, diagnostics, therapy, and post-market surveillance.

The road ahead is far from certain, and GAI-driven drug discovery must continuously prove its worth in the crucible of real-world clinical outcomes. Yet the early successes, coupled with the technology's evident capacity for creativity and iteration, suggest that we are witnessing a watershed moment. The pharmaceutical industry—historically risk-averse and tradition-bound—has begun to embrace GAI's potential to catalyze a new golden age of rapid, precise, and patient-centered innovation. As more GAI-designed therapies reach clinical trials and, eventually, the market, the lessons gleaned from these experiences will set the stage for even more ambitious applications, inching us closer to a future where medicine is at once more scientific and more humane.

Something else currently rocketing us toward that future is the introduction of AI agents, a subject we have touched upon in previous chapters but will take a deeper dive into in our next chapter.

Chapter 10

AI Agents Unlocking the Future of Gen AI for Healthcare

Agents are not only going to change how everyone interacts with computers. They're also going to upend the software industry, bringing about the biggest revolution in computing since we went from typing commands to tapping on icons.

Bill Gates, Co-founder of Microsoft

Throughout this book, we have steadily built a foundation for how generative AI (GAI) is reshaping healthcare, discussing breakthroughs in predictive analytics, drug discovery, synthetic data generation, and the evolving role of multi-agent systems. In particular, Chapters 7 and 8 introduced the concept of **AI agents**—software entities or modules capable of autonomous or semi-autonomous actions—within the healthcare ecosystem. These AI-driven "agents" offer the promise of richer patient engagement, more efficient administrative workflows, and real-time adaptation to ever-changing medical environments.

In this chapter, we will take a deeper look at AI agents and where they stand in the broader context of GAI's evolution. We will explore what makes healthcare an especially potent domain for these autonomous programs, from the strict privacy and compliance requirements that shape their design to the unique communication needs of patients. Drawing on real-world examples, we will highlight the leading players—both established tech

DOI: 10.4324/9781003665434-10

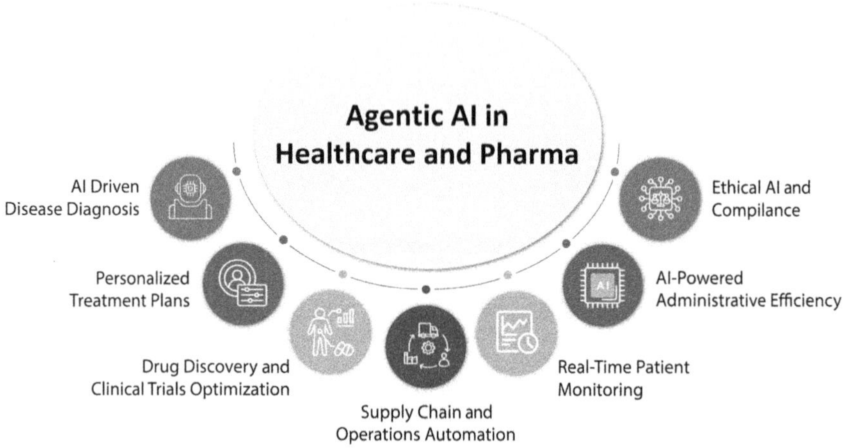

Figure 10.1 How agentic AI is being used in healthcare and pharma. Created by BigRio.

giants and rising stars—who are jockeying to define the future of agent-based AI in healthcare.

Finally, we will address a pivotal question: Is Agentic AI the "next big thing" in healthcare, or is it simply a stepping stone to even more transformative changes? By the end of this chapter, you should have a nuanced understanding of AI agents' current capabilities, challenges, and likely trajectories in a field where human lives, trust, and well-being are paramount. Figure 10.1 illustrates the many touchpoints where Agentic AI can and is impacting healthcare and the pharmaceutical industry.

Understanding AI Agents

An AI agent is a computational system that perceives its environment through sensors (data inputs) and acts upon that environment through effectors (outputs), with the aim of achieving specific goals. Unlike traditional software, which follows a fixed set of instructions, an AI agent is often *autonomous* or semi-autonomous, meaning it can learn or adapt its behaviors based on real-time inputs, user feedback, or historical data. While the concept of an "agent" is not new in computer science, the last decade has seen major strides in reinforcement learning, deep learning, and especially GAI, collectively amplifying these agents' decision-making capabilities and communication skills.

Earlier in the book, we touched on AI agents examining how multi-agent systems coordinate complex tasks in healthcare. A multi-agent system can include multiple specialized AI agents collaborating or even competing to reach optimal outcomes. We also introduced virtual nursing assistants and clinical triage bots as early manifestations of agent technology. Now, we go beyond these initial examples to focus explicitly on the intricacies of AI agents and how they can shape the future of healthcare delivery.

"Here's the exciting reality: many of the Agentic AI-driven tools to radically improve healthcare already exist, especially in their early forms. These tools can mature rapidly with more frequent and diverse usage, and a healthcare company can help make it happen and gain a significant competitive advantage," said Vinod Khosla. "Agentic AI aligns with medicine's mentorship culture. Over the next 5–10 years, it will handle routine tasks—patient intake, preliminary diagnosis, drug titration, chronic disease monitoring, and follow-ups—while doctors supervise, make high-level decisions, and approve care plans."

AI Agents vs. Other Forms of AI

While the boundaries can blur, AI agents differ from other AI-powered applications in three distinct ways:

1. **Autonomy**: An AI agent, ideally, requires minimal human intervention once deployed. For instance, a rule-based system might rely on frequent parameter updates by human operators, whereas a well-designed agent can learn from its interactions, adjusting its strategies or recommendations accordingly.
2. **Goal-Directed Behavior**: AI agents typically operate within a defined set of objectives (e.g., reducing patient wait times, improving patient satisfaction scores) but have the flexibility to find novel solutions, especially if they leverage generative models to propose creative interventions.
3. **Adaptability**: AI agents can refine their approach as conditions change. For instance, a scheduling agent might reconfigure medical staff rosters during a COVID-19 spike based on newly available data, or a triage bot could learn to handle previously unseen symptoms by referencing updated medical guidelines.

The Convergence of Agents and Generative AI

GAI models, which include well-known names like GPT-4 and DALL·E, greatly enhance the potential of AI agents by enabling them to generate entirely new outputs, whether in the form of text, images, or structured data, rather than merely classifying inputs or making predictions. When embedded within an

AI agent architecture, these generative capabilities manifest in several distinct ways. One such way is the agent's ability to conduct highly dynamic dialogues. Instead of confining itself to simple questions and answers, the agent can converse with patients in natural language, clarifying symptoms, offering guidance on self-care, and providing relevant information in real time. Another way GAI augments agents lies in the creation of synthetic data, enabling them to produce realistic patient data that does not compromise privacy. This synthetic data can be useful in simulating rare diseases for research or training purposes, since it avoids exposing identifiable information.

Generative agents can also demonstrate adaptive problem-solving. Drawing from a wide range of medical knowledge, they can propose inventive solutions for operational challenges within healthcare organizations, such as supply chain disruptions or staff scheduling issues. The blend of autonomy, flexible goal-directed behavior, and the ability to generate new solutions or communicate in nuanced ways means that AI agents can address clinical complexity more comprehensively. This synergy between autonomy and generative output forms the core of the next wave of AI in healthcare, enabling these agents to move beyond narrow tasks to more holistic, context-aware responsibilities.

Why Healthcare Is Ripe for Virtual AI Agents

High-Stakes Environment with Complex Workflows

Healthcare presents a layered and high-pressure environment, replete with intricate workflows and far-reaching ethical considerations. Every administrative decision, or lack thereof, carries significant ramifications for patient health. AI agents are uniquely poised to thrive in these conditions because they can process large volumes of real-time data while automatically adapting recommendations in response to changing inputs. Beyond basic data processing, agents can coordinate tasks across multiple departments that may have conflicting schedules or resource constraints. An agent might, for instance, adjust staff rosters when an influx of patients arrives in the emergency department or when hospital admissions surge due to seasonal illnesses. In these moments, the agent's autonomy, combined with an ability to learn from continuous feedback, becomes invaluable. When properly calibrated, agents can enhance efficiency without sacrificing the human oversight that remains critical for safe, empathetic care.

Rita Sharma, Chief Product Officer, Pager Health, shared her insights on why she believes healthcare and AI Agents were made for one another.

"At Pager Health, we're taking a fundamentally different approach to GenAI in healthcare. While most of the industry focuses on narrow applications like scribes, note summarization, and administrative assistance, we're using GenAI-powered agents to solve one of the most pressing challenges in healthcare - bridging the trust gap between patients and the organizations that support them.

Patients place strong trust in their doctors. Seventy-five percent of insured Americans say they rely on their provider to help make care decisions. Health plans play an equally important role, and there is a clear opportunity to build that same level of trust. According to the Pager Health Consumer Experience Survey conducted by The Harris Poll, 76 percent of people say their experience with a health plan directly impacts how much they trust it. As plans continue to improve how they support and engage members, they can strengthen relationships and deliver more trusted and connected care."

Rita went on to explain that this is exactly the issue Pager Health is addressing.

"We've built a modular, extensible AI Agent Directory. It is a system of domain-specific, GenAI-powered virtual agents that guide members through their healthcare journey. These agents don't just answer questions. They support smarter, more seamless navigation across provider search, benefits education, clinical triage, and wellness support. And they do it with context, empathy, and safety guardrails.

This systematized use of agentic AI allows healthcare organizations to become what members want: A trusted partner in care, not just a transactional payer. Our agents deliver on that promise through guiding members with personalized, actionable support that's deeply connected to their benefits and care needs.

In a landscape where most organizations are still experimenting with GenAI on the margins and focused on narrow tasks, Pager Health has built a scalable, operational platform that solves a root cause of dissatisfaction: The erosion of member trust. We're not using GenAI for GenAI's sake. We're using it to make healthcare feel human again."

Stringent Privacy and Compliance Needs

One of the hallmarks of the healthcare industry is the legal framework surrounding patient confidentiality, such as HIPAA in the US or GDPR in the EU. These regulations necessitate strong privacy safeguards, making it imperative for AI agents to incorporate comprehensive data-protection features. This focus on privacy might appear daunting, but it compels AI developers to establish robust security and ethical controls at the core of their designs. When AI agents successfully operate within these frameworks, they instill a sense of confidence in healthcare providers and patients alike. In particular, agents can be engineered to access only the minimal necessary data, leaving a detailed audit trail for regulatory review. They can employ federated learning techniques or advanced encryption schemes to ensure that the patient's data remains protected even when computations involve third-party systems or external analytics services.

Patient Communication and Engagement

Healthcare is not solely about clinical diagnostics and treatments; it is equally about effective communication, education, and patient adherence. This is where virtual AI agents make a substantial impact. They can bridge the gap between clinical encounters by responding to patient inquiries at any time, sending personalized medication reminders, or providing explanations of lab results in accessible language. When integrated with wearable devices, agents can track daily vital signs or activity levels, recognizing worrisome trends and alerting both the patient and healthcare professionals accordingly. Patients appreciate having round-the-clock access to a reliable, knowledgeable interface that offers consistent support and reassurance. By "speaking" multiple languages or adapting content to diverse cultural contexts, AI agents can also cater to patients who might otherwise struggle with traditional, English-only healthcare resources. In doing so, these systems bolster patient engagement and can lead to better adherence to treatment plans, which is increasingly important in value-based healthcare models.

"At Providence, Agentic AI is actively reshaping how the health system interacts with patients," Sara Vaezy, Chief Transformation Officer, Providence told us during an episode of *The Big Unlock.*

She continued, "One compelling example is the development of a conversational and navigation platform designed to fulfill patient needs such as - appointment scheduling, billing support, or financial counseling, without requiring them to message their physician directly. With over six million patient-generated messages annually overwhelming physician inboxes, this platform leverages Agentic AI to recognize intent and activate [voice] agents for task fulfillment. The result is what Providence calls 'message deflection,' reducing unnecessary messages by up to 30%, thus freeing up clinical resources and dramatically improving the patient experience by offering immediate support."

Providence's experience underscores a key insight, GenAI is not just about automating isolated tasks but reimagining entire workflows. For startups, this opens a rich frontier of innovation, particularly in building (Agentic AI) tools that go beyond feature activation and address the full end-to-end patient journey.

Areas such as real-time care navigation, personalized outreach, and AI-driven workflow orchestration present significant opportunities. Additionally, new ventures can play a critical role in developing tools that make non-deterministic AI systems safe and scalable. As Agentic AI becomes integral to healthcare operations, those who focus on augmenting care delivery and operational efficiency at scale will lead the next wave of healthcare transformation.

Real-World Use Cases: AI Agents in Action

Virtual Nursing Assistants

Virtual nursing assistants exemplify how AI agents are already transforming patient care. Often introduced through mobile apps, web portals, or integrated EHR features, these assistants can handle tasks such as medication reminders, plan-of-care updates, and preliminary symptom triage. Rather than merely showing static reminders, some advanced solutions engage in interactive dialogues with patients. A patient might input a concerning symptom, receive an initial recommendation, and then, if the situation seems pressing, be connected directly to a live nurse or physician. The assistant can also transmit real-time data back to the care team, automating alerts when patient-reported symptoms or readings deviate from normal parameters. Companies like Carena, which evolved through acquisitions into larger telehealth ecosystems, have showcased the early potential of such systems. The best of these assistants now incorporate GPT-like natural language capabilities, bringing more conversational fluency and nuanced understanding to their interactions.

AI-Powered Triage and Scheduling

High patient volumes and unpredictable patient inflow place enormous strain on emergency departments and frontline primary care clinics. AI agents attuned to triage can sift through symptom descriptions, medical histories, and even vital signs to assign urgency levels to incoming patients. Such agents expedite care for those who need it most urgently, while ensuring that patients with lower-acuity conditions receive appropriate instructions or schedule follow-ups in a timely manner. This form of triage reduces excessive wait times and alleviates staff workloads. In parallel, scheduling agents harness historical and live data to anticipate patient surges, balancing staff availability across multiple shifts or even multiple facility sites. This capability helps administrators remain agile, reallocating resources to match real-time needs and informing clinicians when they might need to extend their shifts or request additional support from neighboring departments.

Agent-Based Radiology Assistants

The field of radiology has long been on the cutting edge of AI adoption, but agents that organize workflow tasks take this progression further. Instead of merely detecting anomalies in scans, an AI agent can manage the entire process from image capture to final reporting. That might begin with flagging scans that appear to show urgent findings, such as a suspected intracranial hemorrhage, then routing those scans to the radiologist most experienced in neurology. The agent can summarize likely areas of concern, referencing past imaging for comparative purposes and even generating a preliminary report that the radiologist can finalize or modify. Companies like Aidoc pioneered aspects of this approach, and although not wholly agent-based in their early stages, they have begun integrating more automated workflow features. By coupling generative language models with specialized radiology algorithms, future radiology assistants may handle the clerical side of scanning procedures as well, booking follow-ups for any flagged abnormalities, and notifying primary care physicians of the results.

Administrative and Revenue Cycle Agents

Beyond the clinical sphere, administrative complexity has long plagued healthcare systems, contributing to inefficiencies and high costs. Agent-based RPA (Robotic Process Automation) tools offer a remedy by taking on routine tasks like coding, billing, and claims processing. Instead of requiring human coders to pore over lengthy patient charts, an agent can read the relevant clinical notes, identify appropriate billing codes, and submit claims to payers with minimal manual oversight. It can simultaneously check for any inconsistencies or missing pieces of data that might delay processing. Hospitals striving to manage large inventories can also rely on AI agents that track supply usage and reorder essential items in anticipation of upcoming needs, thus minimizing last-minute shortages. Major EHR vendors such as Epic have begun incorporating these automated features, some of which function as behind-the-scenes agents. While these might not always carry the AI label in marketing materials, their agent-like behaviors optimize hospital operations without demanding constant human intervention.

Chatbots and Patient Portals

Although chatbots have sometimes garnered a reputation for oversimplifying customer service interactions, their healthcare applications can be remarkably sophisticated when augmented with generative capabilities and data integration. Patient portals that once showcased static FAQs now offer dynamic dialogues. The system may welcome a patient by name, review their upcoming appointment schedule, and answer specific questions about lab results or treatment plans. A chatbot enhanced with GPT-like text generation can contextualize answers based on the patient's medical history or current prescriptions, producing individualized guidance that surpasses the generic replies of earlier systems. In some instances, these chatbots even escalate to live support if they detect signs that the conversation is moving into critical territory, blending the speed of automated interaction with the emotional sensitivity of human care. Tools such as Ada, Infermedica, and Buoy Health demonstrate how these advanced chatbot models can work with real-time patient data and triage protocols to direct individuals to the correct level of care.

Crystal Broj was happy to share with us the Medical University of South Carolina's successful early adoption of this type of Agentic AI solution.

At MUSC, we've embraced Agentic AI as a core enabler of access, efficiency, and better patient outcomes. One of our most impactful projects has been the launch of "Emily," our 24/7 voice-enabled digital AI Agent. Emily is now live on 42 different phone lines across the organization and handled an impressive 170,000 calls in February alone. This has led to a measurable reduction in call wait times and abandonment rates.

What's even more powerful is what Emily does on those calls:

- *She verified over 2,700 appointments*
- *Cancelled 825 appointments—all without any human intervention*
- *Deflected 17% of total call volume from needing a live agent*
- *Maintained a 3.8 out of 5 satisfaction rating from patients*

That's real value: meeting patients where they are, anytime, while also lightening the operational load on our contact center staff.

Another area we've invested in is with Notable, a GenAI-powered platform we use for multiple automated workflows. We've deployed AI Agent automation for pre-registration, where patients can confirm and update their details before visits. This has helped us reduce manual data entry, increase co-pay collection rates, and lower our no-show rate.

We also use Notable for care-gap outreach, ensuring that patients are reminded about critical screenings and preventative care. And most recently, we began leveraging Notable for prior authorizations. In our initial pilot, 40% of cases were handled entirely without human involvement — a major win, considering how time-consuming and complex that process typically is.

These aren't just pilots or ideas—they're live, scaled solutions that are making a tangible impact today.

Key Players Jockeying for Dominance in AI Agents for Healthcare

Epic Systems

Epic Systems holds a commanding share of the EHR market in the US, making it a pivotal force in the future of AI agents in healthcare. Its expansive user community, which includes both clinicians and patients, gives Epic a platform to roll out agent capabilities to a huge number of hospitals and clinics. Epic's partnerships with AI innovators indicate a growing emphasis on integrating agent-based features directly into the core of its software. MyChart, Epic's patient portal, can incorporate AI chatbots that help patients interpret lab results or schedule follow-up visits. Meanwhile, on the provider side, Epic's In Basket communication tool can be augmented by AI logic that routes messages, identifies urgent inquiries, and drafts preliminary responses for clinicians to review. As a hub for third-party developers, Epic also gives specialized AI startups a ready ecosystem for reaching a wide user base through standardized interfaces and application programming interfaces (APIs).

Google

Google Health, alongside DeepMind, has become a formidable player in AI for healthcare, thanks to extensive experience in machine learning and natural language processing. The company's various AI projects, many derived from its major language model research, empower agent-driven solutions designed to address clinical and operational challenges. Google Cloud's HIPAA-compliant infrastructure and tools allow healthcare organizations to implement Google's agent modules securely. DeepMind's work on advanced reinforcement learning has explored complex tasks like controlling hospital resource usage or predicting patient deterioration, laying a robust foundation for agent strategies. Beyond enterprise-level offerings, Google's footprint in consumer devices and wearables, particularly through its acquisition of Fitbit, could someday extend agent logic directly to the wrists of millions of users. Such a multifaceted approach positions Google to influence every layer of healthcare, from the inpatient setting to personal wellness monitoring.

Salesforce

Although widely recognized for its dominance in customer relationship management (CRM), Salesforce has increasingly gravitated toward healthcare through its Health Cloud offerings and recent investments in AI. The company's Einstein

AI platform, known within the Salesforce ecosystem, applies data analytics and predictive algorithms that can also operate in an agent-like capacity. Healthcare organizations rely on Salesforce to manage patient outreach, follow-up scheduling, and multi-channel communication, creating opportunities for AI agents to unify interactions across phone, email, web chat, and social media. By merging Salesforce's robust CRM backbone with advanced machine learning, healthcare providers can present patients with an integrated experience. Mulesoft, a Salesforce subsidiary specializing in system integration, allows these AI agents to connect disparate data sources across various hospital departments, enabling the agent to assemble a holistic view of the patient journey. While Salesforce might not focus exclusively on clinical outcomes, its ecosystem approach holds considerable weight in administrative and patient engagement domains, areas where AI agents readily prove their worth.

Microsoft

Microsoft has pursued multiple avenues to fortify its standing in healthcare AI. Azure's secure cloud offerings equip hospitals and research institutions with a scalable platform for hosting agent solutions, complete with compliance tools and advanced analytics modules. Through the acquisition of Nuance, a company well-known for clinical documentation and speech recognition, Microsoft now has direct pathways to integrate agent-based intelligence into physician workflows. Rather than simply transcribing encounters, these AI agents can summarize key details, highlight potential red flags, and even expedite order entry or medication reconciliation. Microsoft's integration strategies often revolve around bridging the gap between popular EHR systems and cutting-edge AI toolsets. In addition, the enterprise footprint of Windows and Office ensures that frontline clinicians, who often spend much of their day interacting with Microsoft products, can adopt new agent features in a more frictionless way. Coupled with Microsoft's partnership with OpenAI, which grants it unique access to advanced generative models, the company is well placed to deliver agent solutions across the continuum of care.

Others in the Fray

While Epic, Google, Salesforce, and Microsoft dominate many conversations, the field is crowded with other innovative players. Amazon, for instance, has explored AI-driven healthcare initiatives through AWS cloud services and pilot programs involving Alexa-based virtual care. IBM Watson Health once aimed to revolutionize healthcare with AI-driven decision support, although it has restructured aspects of that division. Specialized telehealth and CRM companies,

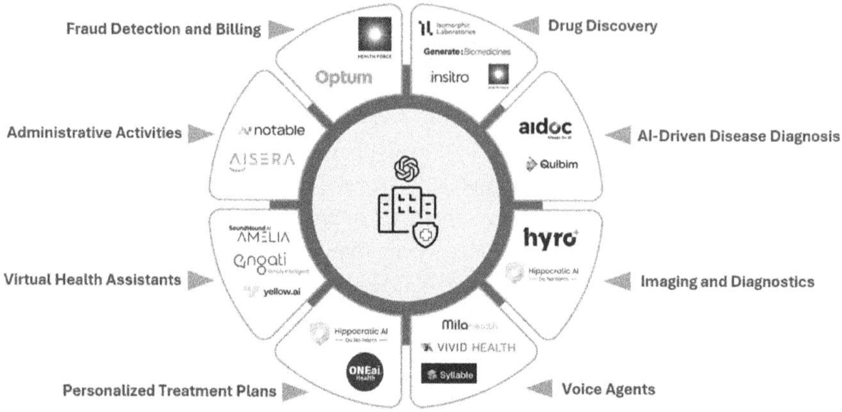

Figure 10.2 Companies that are the key players in Agentic AI and healthcare. Created by BigRio.

including Medallia and various smaller platforms, have embedded agent logic into their products as well. Startups often hone in on specific specialties—mental health, geriatrics, or pediatrics—and build agents tailored to those niches. This fragmented but dynamic landscape ensures that competition and collaboration will continue to fuel rapid innovation in agent-based solutions. Graphic 10.2 illustrates these and several other notable key players in Agentic AI and healthcare and how they are leveraging the technology.

Is Agentic AI "The Next Big Thing" in Healthcare?

The Case for "Yes"

Many industry observers argue that agent-based AI, particularly when powered by sophisticated generative models, is the natural evolution of data-driven healthcare. These agents are capable of scaling operations that would otherwise require large human teams, such as triaging high call volumes or reviewing thousands of diagnostic images overnight. By being able to learn in near real time, AI agents can incorporate fresh research findings or updated clinical guidelines, a critical advantage in medicine, where knowledge expands at a fast pace. Moreover, the value-based care paradigm encourages robust patient engagement and efficient resource usage, both of which are hallmarks of well-implemented AI agents. The synergy with multi-agent systems, where each specialized agent communicates and collaborates with others, points to a future in which entire hospital networks achieve levels of efficiency and insight currently unthinkable.

The Case for Caution

Despite the undeniable potential, caution is warranted. Data quality remains a pervasive issue, and an agent's recommendations are only as good as the information it has consumed. If training data is biased or incomplete, the agent's interventions may inadvertently worsen health disparities or produce unreliable outcomes. Trust and transparency also need careful consideration. Healthcare workers and patients alike may hesitate to rely on an opaque "black box," particularly when an agent's suggestions contradict a known best practice or appear to ignore contextual subtleties. In addition, regulatory bodies have yet to fully catch up with the rapid evolution of AI, leaving questions about liability and formal approval processes. Overreliance on agents can also undermine clinical intuition, which is crucial in emergencies or atypical patient presentations. Indeed, for every productivity gain, there is the possibility that an agent's mistake might be replicated at scale if the system lacks appropriate oversight.

Challenges to Widespread Adoption

Broader adoption of agent-based AI encounters a series of interlocking hurdles. One persistent barrier is interoperability. Healthcare technology ecosystems are often fragmented, with multiple EHRs, lab information systems, and billing platforms. For AI agents to work effectively, they must integrate seamlessly across these disparate technologies—an undertaking that requires standardized data formats, robust APIs, and buy-in from multiple vendors. Another challenge involves the up-front costs and uncertain return on investment. It can be expensive to develop, test, and roll out sophisticated AI agents, leaving smaller clinics or resource-poor health systems at a disadvantage. Cultural resistance also remains a factor. Clinicians who have honed diagnostic or procedural expertise over decades might be reluctant to put their trust in newly introduced "machine intelligence," no matter how rigorously tested. Overcoming these barriers calls for a combination of strong clinical evidence, well-defined regulatory guidelines, and educational initiatives that articulate the agent's role as a collaborator rather than a replacement.

Signs of an Emerging Standard

Although caution is justified, multiple indicators suggest that agent-based AI is gradually maturing into a more standardized approach. Regulatory entities such as the FDA in the US have started developing frameworks for machine learning-driven medical devices, which could eventually include AI agents acting in real time. Professional societies may soon issue guidelines or best practices on integrating AI agents ethically and effectively into workflows, a step that would reassure both clinicians and administrators. Companies like Epic and Microsoft, which enjoy widespread market share, have begun incorporating AI agent features into their default offerings, allowing such technology to expand without hospitals having to do extensive customization. The pace of pilot projects and academic publications exploring agent-based innovations has accelerated. The overall trajectory hints at a future where healthcare professionals view AI agents as necessary infrastructure, just as electronic records and telehealth once progressed from novelty to staple.

Looking Ahead: The Evolving Role of AI Agents

From Reactive to Proactive

Although many current AI agents remain primarily reactive, the shift toward proactive interventions seems inevitable. Instead of waiting for a patient's call to flag worrisome symptoms or for a clinician to initiate a data query, next-generation agents will detect patterns in real time and alert stakeholders before a crisis unfolds. An agent might discern an emerging infection trend within a hospital unit by analyzing lab orders and patient vitals, then recommend proactive precautions or resource allocation. By predicting potential bottlenecks or imminent disease outbreaks, these systems could help healthcare organizations save valuable time and potentially even lives.

Holistic Patient Journeys

As the industry moves away from fragmented care toward more integrated, value-based approaches, AI agents could begin orchestrating the patient's entire healthcare journey. They might monitor wearables, scheduled appointments, medication adherence, and social determinants of health, all at once, to anticipate needs or identify risk factors. Rather than seeing each episode of care in isolation, the agent would connect the dots, ensuring continuity and comprehensiveness. This ability to maintain a cohesive, long-term view of a patient's well-being is crucial for managing chronic illnesses or complex post-operative recoveries and can significantly enhance overall quality of care.

Human-Machine Collaboration

The role of human clinicians will remain indispensable, and AI agents will serve as an augmentative force rather than a substitute. Clinicians will rely on the agent's efficiency and pattern recognition to handle routine analyses or administrative tasks, freeing physicians, nurses, and other staff to exercise higher-order thinking, empathy, and shared decision-making with patients. Meanwhile, the collaborative aspects of multi-agent systems allow for specialized agents that focus on distinct aspects of care, such as diagnosing rare illnesses, optimizing care team scheduling, or ensuring medication adherence, while clinicians supervise and synthesize the insights from these agents to guide patient-centric decisions.

Toward Multi-Agent Ecosystems

Many of the benefits discussed thus far are magnified when multiple agents work in tandem across an entire healthcare network. One agent might excel at resource allocation, another at medication adherence, and a third at triage for emergency departments. They can share relevant insights, provided that data-sharing protocols and privacy measures are robust. The endgame may involve a network in which each hospital floor, outpatient clinic, pharmacy, and even payer system is populated by specialized AI agents collaborating in real time under secure and ethically guided protocols. Achieving this vision depends heavily on open data standards and a shared commitment to responsible AI governance.

Conclusion

AI agents occupy a compelling intersection of autonomy, intelligent decision-making, and the capacity for seamless integration into existing healthcare operations. In healthcare—a field driven by data but grounded in human trust—AI agents must demonstrate reliability, safeguard privacy, and remain transparent enough that clinicians, administrators, and patients can adopt them with confidence. Despite the challenges posed by regulatory constraints, culture shifts, and potential biases in training data, the momentum for agent-based AI adoption continues to grow. Major technology providers such as Epic, Google, Salesforce, and Microsoft are all vying to shape this frontier, leveraging large-scale cloud infrastructures and user-friendly applications.

Looking toward the future, agent-based solutions may shift from their current reactive mode to a more proactive stance, predicting outbreaks, preempting crises, and weaving together patients' journeys so that no gap in care goes unnoticed. Yet there is no scenario, even in the most technologically advanced vision, where AI supplants the wisdom, empathy, and responsibility of human healthcare professionals. The synergy of agents and clinicians, supported by a broader ecosystem of specialized AI solutions, stands as the most likely path forward. Through this collaboration, healthcare can move closer to a reality in which patient outcomes improve, administrative burdens lighten, and the entire care continuum becomes a more efficient and compassionate experience.

Chapter 11

Where We Stand and Where We Dare to Go

Generative AI is teaching us that the way you speak is actually code itself.

Lisa Huang

Generative artificial intelligence (GAI) has emerged as a revolutionary force across healthcare, reshaping diagnostic tools, therapeutic pathways, administrative workflows, and drug discovery. Throughout this book, we have followed GAI's rise from conceptual innovation to practical deployments that bridge patient care, data science, and ethical oversight. As we now conclude, let's look back at our central themes and reflect on the road ahead.

Reaffirming GAI's Transformative Potential

The preceding chapters illustrated how GAI differs fundamentally from earlier generations of AI in healthcare. Traditional machine learning and data analytics often focused on classification or regression tasks that involve assigning labels, detecting anomalies, or making predictions. GAI takes a step further by generating new outputs, whether these are clinical summaries, synthetic patient data, or even novel molecular structures. This creative capacity redefines what computational tools can accomplish in medicine.

Yet, it is crucial to remember that GAI does not act in isolation. Rather, it augments and interacts with the expertise of clinicians, researchers, and administrators. Throughout the chapters, we have seen how the technology can help

DOI: 10.4324/9781003665434-11

detect disease earlier, propose more personalized treatments, and streamline administrative tasks, all while maintaining or improving patient outcomes. In many respects, GAI lifts the burden of routine or repetitive tasks so healthcare professionals can focus more sharply on direct patient interactions, diagnostics, and other high-level decision-making.

Reflecting on diagnostics, for instance, GAI-assisted systems have shown promise in reading and interpreting imaging scans, scanning medical records for patterns invisible to the human eye, and reducing diagnostic errors. When it comes to treatment, generative models can adapt medication regimens for each patient, predicting side effects or identifying ideal dosage levels based on massive datasets. Even in administrative realms such as resource allocation or discharge planning, GAI helps institutions cut costs, optimize staffing, and minimize operational inefficiencies.

In the realm of research and drug discovery, generative models can envision molecules beyond existing chemical libraries. Pharmaceutical companies now have the capability to compress what used to be years of molecular exploration into months or even weeks. The speed gains, combined with improved accuracy, translate into potentially life-saving therapies reaching patients more quickly. Across all these domains, GAI acts as an amplifier of human ingenuity rather than a substitute for it, reinforcing the overarching narrative that the marriage of advanced AI and clinical expertise propels healthcare toward a more efficient, patient-centric future.

Revisiting the Key Themes and Achievements

Reviewing the milestones covered in this book, it is evident that GAI excels at identifying and exploiting correlations that would otherwise escape notice. Human cognition, while extraordinarily flexible, is bounded by biological constraints—attention, memory, and susceptibility to bias. GAI systems, in contrast, thrive on large-scale data ingestion and pattern recognition, especially when generating new hypotheses or proposals.

In earlier chapters, we highlighted how GAI streamlines diagnoses by recognizing subtle signals, such as minute irregularities on diagnostic images or hidden relationships in patient histories. When harnessed responsibly, these capabilities push the boundaries of what clinicians can do within their time and mental bandwidth. We also saw how the technology can automate the generation of clinical notes, saving physicians from hours of manual documentation. The example of ambient listening systems underscored how these breakthroughs transition from "interesting ideas" to "must-have tools" in a relatively short span, particularly once frontline clinicians experience tangible benefits.

Another key takeaway is GAI's role in reshaping drug discovery. Where earlier computational methods relied heavily on screening existing compounds, generative algorithms can propose entirely new scaffolds and test them in silico against a target protein's structure. This creative leap, coupled with real-world validation, opens new frontiers in the fight against complex diseases. Historically, drug development has been notoriously expensive and time-consuming, requiring extensive trial-and-error cycles. GAI compresses these cycles by intelligently predicting which chemical configurations offer the highest likelihood of therapeutic success, greatly reducing unnecessary experiments.

Throughout these advancements, a recurrent theme has been the necessity of education and careful oversight. Clinicians, nurses, pharmacists, and administrative staff need adequate training not only in how to operate AI tools but also in how to critique and interpret algorithmic outputs. Likewise, accountability structures must be clear so that when errors occur—or biases surface—institutions can respond in a transparent and corrective manner. The appointment of positions like the Chief AI Officer (CAIO) is one response to this need for governance and strategic oversight, ensuring that AI projects align with institutional goals and regulatory requirements.

Ethics and equity remain at the forefront of discussions about GAI's integration into healthcare. Stakeholders must confront the risks of algorithmic bias, data privacy breaches, and the potential to exacerbate existing health disparities. However, when approached thoughtfully, GAI can reduce rather than increase such disparities by improving access to quality diagnostics and treatments, especially in underserved communities. That said, realization of this positive outcome hinges on deliberate design choices, ongoing audits, and responsible deployment strategies that prioritize fairness.

The Current Market and Future Investment

Even as Gen AI continues to prove its worth in clinical diagnostics, drug discovery, and operational efficiencies, a parallel story is unfolding in the world of venture capital, corporate strategy, and governmental funding initiatives. Over the past several years, investors have shown unprecedented enthusiasm for AI in healthcare, with a growing share of this attention devoted specifically to GAI. A convergence of factors—maturing algorithms, reduced computing costs, and heightened demand for innovative healthcare solutions—has propelled GAI from a niche research topic to a lucrative investment category.

Analysts have documented a steep climb in funding for AI-driven healthcare startups over the last decade, with annual global investments in digital health and biotech-related AI exceeding tens of billions of dollars. Within that broad

AI-in-healthcare domain, generative models—capable of creating new molecular structures, drafting clinical documentation, or producing synthetic data—have been attracting particularly robust funding since around 2018. Venture capital firms and technology giants alike see GAI as a catalyzing force with the potential to shave years off drug development timelines, drastically cut healthcare operating costs, and open up entirely new business lines in data monetization, clinical trial management, and personalized medicine.

Recent market reports suggest that global investments in GAI-powered healthcare solutions reached a multi-billion-dollar figure by the early 2020s, with an array of new entrants each year and established tech behemoths expanding their healthcare portfolios. Funding often takes the form of seed or Series A rounds for emerging GAI-based startups, while more mature companies have closed Series B and Series C rounds well into the hundreds of millions. In parallel, public-private partnerships—involving academic institutions, government agencies, and industry leaders—have emerged to address grand-scale objectives like pandemic preparedness and national AI strategies, further fueling capital inflows.

Looking forward, market analysts project a robust Compound Annual Growth Rate (CAGR) for AI in healthcare, particularly in the GAI segment, that could exceed 35–40% through 2030. Multiple drivers underpin this optimistic forecast. First, demographic pressures and rising healthcare expenditures create a fertile environment for solutions that can streamline patient care and reduce operational overhead. Second, the pharmaceutical industry's sustained interest in generative models for drug design and development has led to high-profile success stories, most notably those that accelerated COVID-19 vaccine research, validating GAI's potential for rapid clinical impact. Third, many healthcare providers and hospital systems have recognized the strategic advantage of investing in AI to cope with workforce shortages, staff burnout, and the ever-growing volume of medical data that no human can reliably sift through without computational assistance.

Despite this optimistic outlook, investors often note challenges that may influence the pace of adoption. Regulatory uncertainty, data privacy constraints, and ethical considerations can slow down or complicate large-scale deployments. Skill shortages, especially in the intersectional areas of AI, medicine, and data science, mean organizations must also invest heavily in talent acquisition and training. Nonetheless, these headwinds have so far done little to dampen overall enthusiasm. Rather, they accentuate the likelihood that the next wave of winning GAI companies will be those that navigate these complexities effectively, forming well-structured collaborations with healthcare providers, pharmaceutical firms, and regulatory bodies.

Taken together, these trends point to an investment landscape where GAI is increasingly viewed as a cornerstone of the healthcare sector's digital transformation. The trajectory of funding and the projected CAGR through 2030 indicate that GAI's current footprint in healthcare is only the beginning of a much larger growth trajectory. Companies, researchers, and policymakers that seize these opportunities—while maintaining a keen awareness of clinical efficacy, safety, and equity—stand to shape the future of medicine in ways that will resonate well beyond the financial markets, transforming patient experiences and outcomes on a global scale.

The Next Frontier: Agentic AI in Healthcare

Although GAI's creative capabilities mark a transformational stage in healthcare, the technological evolution does not end here. As we addressed in our last chapter, "Agentic AI" is a concept gaining increasing attention. Instead of merely taking commands and producing content, AI agents represent a more autonomous or semi-autonomous extension of generative capabilities. Agent AI systems can proactively orchestrate a series of tasks, coordinate multiple specialized AI modules, and manage real-time data streams across an organization.

Consider how a single hospital might use Agentic AI. It could continuously analyze emergency department volumes, staff schedules, medication inventories, and even local epidemiological trends, making adjustments as needed to optimize resource usage. Alternatively, in a drug discovery context, an Agent AI could oversee the entire pipeline—from hypothesizing target proteins to vetting novel compounds for toxicity, coordinating synthetic routes, and even designing adaptive clinical trial protocols. The synergy among different AI modules—each focused on tasks like protein structure prediction, patient stratification, or supply chain logistics—comes under one unified "Agent Coordinator" that orchestrates workflows with minimal human intervention.

This coordinated approach promises to eliminate fragmentation and inefficiencies that often arise in large, complex healthcare systems. Yet it also raises the stakes. While GAI can generate outputs that a human expert evaluates, Agentic AI platforms might be authorized to make certain real-time decisions—rerouting patients to a less crowded hospital unit, for example, or authorizing dosage adjustments based on immediate data feedback. Such autonomy demands rigorous safeguards, interpretability standards, and fail-safe protocols to ensure that mistakes or biases do not cascade unchecked. Clear lines of accountability become paramount, and so do robust governance frameworks that define how an agent-based system interacts with clinicians, patients, and administrators.

Proponents of Agentic AI see it as the logical next step in healthcare automation: a system that can manage complexity more adeptly than any single person or even a team of experts, all without sacrificing the nuance and ethical oversight that comes from continuous human involvement. The concept envisions healthcare not as a collection of siloed departments but as a dynamically integrated ecosystem, with the Agentic AI seamlessly coordinating the flow of patients, information, and resources. The result could be a more unified, responsive, and data-driven healthcare model.

Still, the potential pitfalls discussed in Chapter 10 cannot be overlooked. A system that coordinates critical decisions across multiple domains—financial, clinical, and administrative—could amplify any inherent bias or algorithmic blind spot. Addressing these challenges will necessitate evolving best practices in validation, audit trails, and interoperability. The foundational questions remain: How do we maintain transparent communication with end-users, from nurses to surgeons to the general public? How do we handle liability if an AI Agent's decisions lead to negative outcomes? And how might we ensure that these systems remain accessible and equitable rather than perpetuating inequalities in healthcare delivery?

Responsible Development and Deployment

The conversation about GAI in healthcare cannot conclude without reiterating the importance of responsible innovation. Every piece of technology introduced into patient care carries ethical implications, some of which may not be immediately evident. GAI amplifies those implications due to its ability to generate original outputs that clinicians might adopt with minimal scrutiny, especially if a model's recommendations appear consistently accurate at first glance.

A robust framework for responsible deployment addresses multiple layers. First, data transparency and privacy must be upheld. Even if generative models use synthetic patient data for training, that data's characteristics must be representative of real demographics, ensuring that marginalized populations are not left out. Second, interpretability and explainability are critical when an AI tool suggests diagnoses, treatments, or operational changes. Clinicians have a right—and a responsibility—to know why a model made a particular recommendation, especially when patient safety is on the line.

Third, bias mitigation should remain a constant priority. If a model is not regularly audited for bias in outcomes or performance discrepancies among different patient groups, it may inadvertently exacerbate health disparities. Fourth, a thorough and transparent validation process is essential. Potential best practices include external peer review, multi-institutional collaborations, and continuous performance monitoring in real-world settings. This helps to confirm not only the efficacy of GAI solutions but also their reliability and fairness. Finally, fostering interdisciplinary partnerships among clinicians, data scientists, ethicists, and policymakers can ensure that the full spectrum of perspectives is represented in any GAI deployment.

Although the challenges are substantial, so are the opportunities. Properly guided, GAI can significantly reduce administrative burdens, democratize access to quality care, and streamline research in ways previously unimaginable. The financial implications are also non-trivial; efficiently leveraging GAI may lower operational costs, reduce unnecessary procedures, and direct resources to areas of greatest need. This confluence of clinical, ethical, and economic factors underscores why so many healthcare organizations have begun to treat AI not as a speculative curiosity but as a strategic imperative.

Looking to the Future: Encouraging Continued Innovation

As we peer into the horizon, the trajectory of GAI in healthcare appears both exhilarating and complex. A recurring note in earlier chapters is that GAI and other AI forms are not stagnant technologies; they evolve rapidly as new research and computational paradigms emerge. One year might see breakthroughs in generative image synthesis that help with radiology, while another could bring quantum computing advances that supercharge molecular modeling. In parallel, regulatory bodies are adapting to ensure that new capabilities align with safety and accountability.

The longevity of GAI's impact hinges on the sustained commitment of multiple stakeholders. Clinicians who interact with AI-driven systems must maintain a critical mindset, asking hard questions about algorithmic limitations. Healthcare administrators and policy leaders should continue refining frameworks that balance innovation with patient well-being. Researchers, whether in academia or industry, will push the boundaries of what is possible with generative models, from advanced protein folding to personalized vaccine development. Each of these efforts requires long-term funding, robust data infrastructures, and progressive educational initiatives that cultivate AI literacy among medical professionals.

This is where the broader community of innovators comes in—entrepreneurs, nonprofit organizations, government agencies, and large healthcare institutions all have roles to play. Startups can rapidly develop and test new GAI prototypes, while large institutions can integrate those solutions at scale, yielding invaluable real-world feedback. Professional associations can sponsor conferences, workshops, and continuing education modules that keep healthcare providers at the leading edge of AI knowledge. Governments can incentivize research through grants, offering tax breaks, or streamlined regulatory pathways that stimulate further experimentation.

Given the global scope of healthcare, international collaborations and data-sharing initiatives may prove decisive in accelerating advancements. By pooling resources, expertise, and diverse patient data sets, multinational coalitions could turbocharge the learning cycles of GAI systems. Cross-border consortia have already begun forming around topics like cancer genomics and rare disease research. Incorporating GAI into these collaborations will likely amplify the pace and scale of discoveries, especially if ethical considerations and equitable benefits remain part of the guiding principles.

To this end, we have created a Center of Excellence and GAI-Innovation Hub in India that Ritu heads up. India is an ideal setting for a GAI Innovation Hub. The Indian government, its universities, and its banking and financial sectors are all in great support of the development of high-tech, with a focus on creating AI-centric opportunities. Our GAI Innovation Hub will be focused on building teams that can show corporate executives what GAI is, what it can do, and how it might enable new business models and strategies. The goal in creating the Hub was to provide a unique talent pool for our US clients while at the same time supporting GAI education and advancement in India. To date, from PoCs to pilot projects, these teams have resulted in significant cost savings and an accelerated pace of GAI development for our clients.

Even as we celebrate the leaps in generative design and real-time analytics, we should remember that GAI's core value proposition remains deeply human in its essence. Its ability to reduce physician burnout, enhance patient outcomes, and elevate the overall quality of care resonates because it aligns with the ethical pillars of medicine. Far from replacing the compassion, empathy, and clinical acumen that define patient care, GAI gives healthcare professionals more bandwidth to exercise those virtues. Ultimately, technology is a tool, not an end. The driving question remains: How do we harness GAI's computational brilliance to uphold—and even deepen—the practice of medicine as a profoundly human endeavor?

Final Thoughts: Writing the Next Chapter on AI and Healthcare

One look at today's headlines and it is easy to see that many Americans feel frustrated with a healthcare system that seems broken and plagued by systemic inefficiencies. The government, the private sector, and medical consumers themselves are spending so much on healthcare, and yet, average people are not reaping the benefits in better outcomes. Is GAI a cure-all for all that is broken? No. But it can provide a lot of fixes in both the near and long term.

The government, the private sector, and medical consumers themselves are spending so much on healthcare, and yet, average people are not reaping the benefits in better outcomes. Is GAI a cure-all for all that is broken? No. But it can provide a lot of fixes in both the near and long term.

In traversing the chapters of this book, we have illuminated the vast and varied terrain GAI occupies in contemporary healthcare. From diagnosing rare diseases with uncanny accuracy to accelerating the drug discovery timeline, from tailoring treatment regimens to creating synthetic data for safer collaborative research, GAI's touch is evident at every juncture. These achievements underscore both the promise and the responsibility that come with unleashing computational creativity in domains where human lives hang in the balance.

The final note of our narrative concerns the future, particularly how GAI might transition into the world of Agentic AI, a technology capable of overseeing multiple, interlinked processes with minimal human intervention. While these agent-based systems can deliver unprecedented efficiencies, they also raise complex ethical, legal, and organizational questions. As with any evolution in healthcare technology, the key lies in ensuring that fundamental medical ethics—beneficence, nonmaleficence, autonomy, and justice—guide every step.

Looking back, it is clear that the adoption of GAI is not a simple technological upgrade but a paradigm shift. From the vantage point of clinicians, the shift promises liberation from repetitive tasks and an expanded scope of diagnostic insight. For administrators, it signals improved resource allocation, operational efficiencies, and cost containment. For researchers and pharmaceutical companies, GAI shortens the timeline between concept and clinical trial, potentially saving millions of dollars and countless lives in the long run.

Yet this integration cannot and should not be rushed. Carefully managed pilot projects, robust training programs, interdisciplinary collaborations, and transparent stakeholder communication all stand out as critical enablers. Institutions that cultivate an environment of continuous learning, openness to feedback, and a willingness to iterate on AI-related processes will be best positioned to harness the full transformative power of GAI.

Ultimately, the genuine revolution GAI ushers in is not just about advanced algorithms or new devices; it is about a reimagining of how medical knowledge is generated, shared, and applied. In the hands of skilled clinicians and thoughtful administrators, GAI can precipitate a golden era of medical innovation, one in which patient outcomes, economic feasibility, and ethical considerations can be simultaneously optimized rather than relegated to compromise.

To close, we return to a sentiment threaded throughout these chapters: GAI stands at the frontier of possibility precisely because it augments human intuition with computational depth. By capitalizing on massive datasets and creative modeling, it reconfigures the boundaries of what is feasible in clinical care and drug development. As the technology continues to evolve, new chapters in its story will unfold—chapters detailing the widespread deployment of ambient technologies, the integration of Agentic AI to unify complex healthcare systems and solve interoperability issues, and the expansion of precision medicine to unprecedented levels of granularity.

In the face of such novelty, the stakes are undeniably high. Stakeholders have the opportunity—and the responsibility—to champion GAI deployments that widen access to care, uplift underserved communities, and maintain a steadfast commitment to patient welfare. Our hope is that this book has provided not only a comprehensive overview of GAI in healthcare but also a spark of inspiration and a practical guide for the countless innovators, clinicians, researchers, policymakers, and entrepreneurs who stand at the threshold of this exciting new era.

The closing of this volume, then, is less a conclusion than a beginning—an invitation to shape the future of healthcare by embracing the gifts of generative intelligence, guided at every turn by a moral compass focused on the shared pursuit of elevating humanity to unprecedented heights.

Index

Note: *Italic* page numbers refer to figures.

For Product Safety Concerns and Information please contact our EU
representative GPSR@taylorandfrancis.com
Taylor & Francis Verlag GmbH, Kaufingerstraße 24, 80331 München, Germany

www.ingramcontent.com/pod-product-compliance
Ingram Content Group UK Ltd.
Pitfield, Milton Keynes, MK11 3LW, UK
UKHW022119190926
475702UK00013B/1539
* 9 7 8 1 0 4 1 1 2 5 6 7 9 *